Henry Blackburn, Gustave Doré

**The Pyrenees**

A Description of Summer Life at French Watering Places

Henry Blackburn, Gustave Doré

**The Pyrenees**
*A Description of Summer Life at French Watering Places*

ISBN/EAN: 9783337407537

Printed in Europe, USA, Canada, Australia, Japan

Cover: Foto ©Andreas Hilbeck / pixelio.de

More available books at **www.hansebooks.com**

A BREAK IN THE PINE FOREST

# THE PYRENEES

ILLUSTRATED BY
GUSTAVE DORÉ.

THE

# PYRENEES:

A DESCRIPTION OF

*Summer Life at French Watering Places.*

BY

## HENRY BLACKBURN,

EDITOR OF 'ACADEMY NOTES;'
AUTHOR OF 'ARTISTS AND ARABS,' 'BRETON FOLK,'
'ART IN THE MOUNTAINS,' ETC.

'Les Pyrénées sont la bordure gracieuse d'un paysage riant et d'un ciel magnifique; la beauté ici est sereine, et le plaisir est pur.'

*NEW EDITION, REVISED AND CORRECTED TO 1880.*

WITH

ONE HUNDRED ILLUSTRATIONS BY GUSTAVE DORÉ,
AND A NEW MAP OF ROUTES FOR TRAVELLERS.

# PREFACE.

IN the present volume it is proposed to describe, in familiar language, the scenery and summer life, in the Pyrenees, arranged in the form of a tour or visit, to the most popular places; and to do this as completely as possible, the Author has permission to introduce a few extracts from the work of a French writer.

M. Taine's remarks, independently of their humour and picturesque grace, have a peculiar value in these pages, in giving the reader an assurance that 'summer life in the Pyrenees' is not represented from a one-sided point of view. In a few words introduced here and there, it will be seen that, whilst delighting in satirising his own countrymen, he thoroughly appreciates the beauties of nature, and enjoys the sunshine of the Pyrenees as much as any Briton. 'On a pris,' he says, 'l'amour de la vie avec l'amour de la lumière,' and sympathetically asks, 'Combien de fois, sous le ciel nébuleux du Nord, formons-nous un pareil désir?'

With regard to the Illustrations, it is scarcely too much to say that the drawings by M. Doré (more than one hundred in number) form, as a whole, the most perfect picture of the Pyrenees ever presented to the public, and bring home to us the features of beautiful mountains, with which Englishmen are strangely unfamiliar.

Amongst the special additions to this Edition (much of which has been rewritten), are descriptions of Lourdes and Argelès in 1880, and some notes made in 'spring amongst the flowers.'

In the Map at the end of the Volume, the routes described have been laid down; and in the APPENDIX will be found the latest information for travellers in the Pyrenees.

LONDON, *October*, 1880.

# CONTENTS.

| | | PAGE |
|---|---|---|
| CHAP. | I.—BORDEAUX—THE LANDES—DAX—ORTHEZ | 1 |
| ,, | II.—PAU | 15 |
| ,, | III.—VAL D'OSSAU—EAUX-CHAUDES | 30 |
| ,, | IV.—EAUX-BONNES | 60 |
| ,, | V.—LOURDES—ARGELÈS—CAUTERETS | 86 |
| ,, | VI.—STORM | 112 |
| ,, | VII.—VAL DE LUZ—CHAOS—GAVARNIE—BRÈCHE DE ROLAND | 121 |
| ,, | VIII.—LUZ—ST. SAUVEUR—BARÈGES—BAGNÈRES DE BIGORRE | 144 |
| ,, | IX.—LUCHON | 163 |
| ,, | X.—VALLÉE DU LYS—LAC D'OO—LE PORT DE VENASQUE | 185 |
| ,, | XI.—ST. BERTRAND DE COMMINGES—TOULOUSE | 208 |
| ,, | XII.—BAYONNE—BIARRITZ—ST. JEAN DE LUZ | 226 |
| | FLOWERS IN THE PYRENEES | 241 |
| NEW MAP OF ROUTES | | face 246 |

## APPENDIX.

LIST OF WATERING PLACES, AND INFORMATION FOR TRAVELLERS, CORRECTED TO 1880 .. .. .. 247

# LIST OF ILLUSTRATIONS.

A BREAK IN THE PINE FOREST .. .. .. .. .. .. *Frontispiece.*
THE VAL D'OSSAU .. .. .. .. .. .. .. .. .. *Vignette.*

|  |  | PAGE |
|---|---|---|
| CHAP. I.—The Gave | .. .. .. .. .. .. .. .. .. | 1 |
| ,, | Shipping at Bordeaux .. .. .. .. .. .. .. | 5 |
| ,, | The Landes .. .. .. .. .. .. .. .. .. | 7 |
| ,, | ,, .. .. .. .. .. .. .. .. .. | 9 |
| ,, | Dax .. .. .. .. .. .. .. .. .. | 10 |
| ,, | ,, .. .. .. .. .. .. .. .. .. | 11 |
| ,, | Orthez .. .. .. .. .. .. .. .. .. | 13 |
| CHAP II.—View from Pau | .. .. .. .. .. .. .. .. | 16 |
| ,, | The Château.. .. .. .. .. .. .. .. | 18 |
| ,, | The Park .. .. .. .. .. .. .. .. | 22 |
| ,, | Courtyard of the Château .. .. .. .. .. | 23 |
| ,, | General view of Pau . .. .. .. .. .. .. | 25 |
| CHAP. III.—View in the Val d'Ossau | .. .. .. .. .. .. | 31 |
| ,, | ,, ,, .. .. .. .. .. .. | 32 |
| ,, | Inhabitants of the Val d'Ossau .. .. .. .. | 33 |
| ,, | Distant view of the Pic du Midi .. .. .. .. | 34 |
| ,, | View in the Val d'Ossau .. .. .. .. .. | 37 |
| ,, | A Sketch in Church .. .. .. .. .. .. | 42 |
| ,, | Route to Eaux-Chaudes .. .. .. .. .. | 47 |
| ,, | ,, ,, .. .. .. .. .. .. | 49 |
| ,, | Environs of Eaux-Chaudes.. .. .. .. .. | 51 |
| ,, | Valley above Gabas .. .. .. .. .. .. | 53 |

# LIST OF ILLUSTRATIONS.

CHAP. III. (*continued*).

|  |  | PAGE |
|---|---|---|
| ,, | Evening near Gabas | 55 |
| ,, | The Blind Fiddler | 56 |
| ,, | Col de Gourzy after a Storm | 58 |

CHAP. IV.—Mountains near Eaux-Bonnes ... 61
,, The Pic de Ger ... 63
,, Sunset on the Mountains ... 69
,, Clouds and Peaks ... 70
,, Invalids taking the waters ... 71
,, The German Band ... 72
,, 'En Queue' ... 73
,, Cascade du Valentin ... 75
,, A Cascade ... 76
,, Cascade du Valentin ... 79
,, ,, ,, ... 80
,, The Home of Wild Flowers ... 81
,, The Pic de Ger ... 82

CHAP. V.—Lourdes ... 88
,, View near Argelès ... 93
,, Part of the Val de Luz ... 95
,, Cauterets ... 97
,, A Mountaineer ... 99
,, Cascade near the Pont d'Espagne ... 101
,, The Pont d'Espagne ... 103
,, The Lac de Gaube ... 105
,, A Dancing Bear ... 110

CHAP. VI.—Storm ... 114
,, The Battle of the Trees ... 116
,, The Gave after a Storm ... 118
,, ,, ,, ... 119

CHAP. VII.—The Gorge de Pierrefitte ... 122
,, St. Sauveur ... 123
,, A Bird's-eye View ... 124
,, Old Bridge at Scia ... 127
,, Chaos ... 128
,, Gèdres ... 129
,, Chaos ... 133

# LIST OF ILLUSTRATIONS. xiii

CHAP. VII. (*continued*). PAGE
- Cirque de Gavarnie .. .. .. .. .. .. .. .. 136
- ,, ,, .. .. .. .. .. .. .. 137
- Cascades .. .. .. .. .. .. .. .. .. 139
- Ascent of the Pic de Bergons.. .. .. .. .. .. 141
- Ascending and descending .. .. .. .. .. .. 143

CHAP. VIII.—Ancient Church of the Templars at Luz .. .. .. 144
- Château near Luz .. .. .. .. .. .. .. .. 145
- The Gave, near Luz .. .. .. .. .. .. .. 146
- View of the Gave. (Sunset) .. .. .. .. .. .. 147
- At Luz .. .. .. .. .. .. .. .. .. 148
- Barèges .. .. .. .. .. .. .. .. .. 149
- Summer Visitors .. .. .. .. .. .. .. .. 150
- Winter Visitors .. .. .. .. .. .. .. .. 151
- A Winter Scene .. .. .. .. .. .. .. .. 152
- 'Un Ascension' .. .. .. .. .. .. .. .. 154
- The Mountains.. .. .. .. .. .. .. .. .. 156
- Pine Trees.. .. .. .. .. .. .. .. .. 157
- The Woods above Bigorre .. .. .. .. .. .. 161

CHAP. IX.—Luchon .. .. .. .. .. .. .. .. .. 164
- Valley of Luchon .. .. .. .. .. .. .. .. 165
- Environs of Luchon.. .. .. .. .. .. .. .. 167
- Path leading to Super-Bagnères .. .. .. .. .. 171
- A 'baigneur' .. .. .. .. .. .. .. .. .. 176
- Dîner .. .. .. .. .. .. .. .. .. .. 177
- The Woods near Luchon .. .. .. .. .. .. 183

CHAP. X.—A Summer Shower .. .. .. .. .. .. .. 187
- Cascades .. .. .. .. .. .. .. .. .. 191
- A Procession .. .. .. .. .. .. .. .. 196
- The Lac d'Oo .. .. .. .. .. .. .. .. 197
- Route to Port de Venasque .. .. .. .. .. .. 200
- ,, ,, .. .. .. .. .. 201
- The Maladetta .. .. .. .. .. .. .. .. 203
- The Port de Venasque (from the south) .. .. .. 204
- Through the Woods .. .. .. .. .. .. .. 206

CHAP. XI.—The Valley after rain .. .. .. .. .. .. 209
- En route to Toulouse .. .. .. .. .. .. .. 210

## LIST OF ILLUSTRATIONS.

CHAP. XI. (*continued*).
,, St. Bertrand de Comminges .. .. ..
,, St. Sernin .. .. .. .. .. .. ..
,, St. Etienne .. .. . .. .. .. ..
,, Toulouse .. .. .. .. .. .. ..
,, Cloisters at the Museum .. .. .. ..
,, Tarbes.. .. .. .. .. .. .. ..
,, Bayonne .. .. .. .. .. .. ..

CHAP. XII.—Villa Eugénie .. .. .. .. .. ..
,, A Natural Bridge .. .. .. .. ..
,, The Coast near Biarritz .. .. .. ..
,, ,, ,, ,, .. .. .. ..
,, Near St. Jean de Luz.. .. .. .. ..

# THE PYRENEES.

### CHAPTER I.

*BORDEAUX—LES LANDES—DAX—ORTHEZ.*

'Je te salue, ô nature fleurie,
　Ton doux aspect vient ranimer mon cœur :
　O viens charmer, viens embellir ma vie,
　Et dans mon âme apporter le bonheur !'

IN the early days of summer—when the streets of Paris begin to have a deserted appearance, and there is scarcely a chair to be had on the ride in the Bois de Boulogne at the fashionable hour ; when '*Les Grandes Eaux*' at Versailles, or a 'dîner particulier' at Enghien, with moonlight boating on the lake afterwards, attract more visitors than the theatres or the sights of the town—a little journal puts forth its leaves, and finds its way into the principal salons and cafés of Paris. It is called the '*Moniteur des Eaux*,' and its mission is to set forth, in glowing colours, the attractions of the various watering-places of France, and to suggest to the weary, or invalid Parisian, where he may find recreation, and drink the waters of health.

Its outward appearance and illustrations are suggestive and enticing, redolent of sea air and mountain breezes. On the title-page there is a picture of an ideal watering-place, in which every conceivable costume (or absence of costume) is suggested, either for the mountains, the sands, or the sea ; the illustration being surrounded by a border of oyster-shells, festooned with sea-weed. In the centre of each shell is a little vignette view of Ems, Étretat, or other well-known summer resort, and the page is completed by other imaginative pictures of horse-races, boat-races, mountains, cascades, and waterfalls, and above all, by a view of a great crowd, besieging the '*Office des Eaux*,' in Paris, where particulars about accommodation at French watering-places are to be obtained.

The catalogue of attractions reads well, and we have every assurance, that whether we seek sea breezes, or a sojourn amongst the mountains of the Pyrenees, we shall be well cared for, and 'on moderate terms ;' thus at Biarritz we are offered :—

'HABITATIONS ET HÔTELS POUR TOUTES LES FORTUNES. Trois belles plages sablonneuses à des expositions différentes où la mer présente une action variée. Beaux établissements de bains, confortables, bien installés, administrés par la commune. La station de bains la plus recherchée et la plus agréable de tout le littoral de l'Océan.'

In the Pyrenees, at Bagnères de Bigorre (a watering-place, nearly 2000 feet above sea-level, but easily approached by railway), the invalid, or the *ennuyé*, will find every comfort and convenience, thus :—

'Eaux salines, ferrugineuses, arsénicales, en boisson ; bains et douches de toute forme.—Eau sulfureuse en boisson et bains à l'hydrofère.—*Vaporarium* complet et étuves, bains russes—Casino et musique au parc tous les jours.—Salon de conversation.—BALS et CONCERTS.—THÉÂTRE.—PROMENADES.—Bonnes voitures et chevaux de montagnes.—Le tout à des *prix inférieurs* à ceux des autres stations thermales des Pyrénées.'

The list in the *Moniteur* includes nearly every sea-bathing place on the coast, and all the mineral watering-places of France; but as we are going southward, we are chiefly interested in those headed '*Pyrenees.*'

Under this title we find special mention made of—

PAU, EAUX-CHAUDES, EAUX-BONNES, CAUTERETS, GAVARNIE, LUZ, ST. SAUVEUR, BARÈGES, BAGNÈRES DE BIGORRE, LUCHON, and BIARRITZ,

and it is to these places that we are about to conduct the reader. They represent, in fact, a short tour that may be called, for want of a better name, the 'regular round;' comprehending, in themselves and their environs, some of the most beautiful spots on the French side of the Pyrenees.

In the map which accompanies this volume, we have indicated the route—approaching the Pyrenees by Bordeaux and Pau, confining ourselves almost exclusively to the French side of the mountains, and taking Biarritz and St. Jean de Luz, on our homeward journey.

The Pyrenees extend for about 260 miles from west to east, and the average height of this continuous chain of mountains is about 6000 feet. They reach in one almost unbroken line from the Bay of Biscay to the Mediterranean, standing like a wall between France and Spain; a natural barrier against friends or foes, especially effective in repressing the 'advance of civilisation,' from which Spain is so much averse, and which it is the ambition and the pride of France to spread in other directions.

It is difficult to cross into Spain, excepting at the extreme ends of this chain, where the mountains slope down to the sea, but there are numerous passes, or '*Ports*,' as they are expressively called, at the heads of the valleys, which Spanish smugglers know well, and through which travellers, on foot or on horseback, may easily cross the frontier.

The valleys by which the northern side of the Pyrenees is approached, are generally from 25 to 30 miles long, running nearly parallel to each other in a southerly direction, and each terminating in a 'cul de sac,' which necessitates a tiresome return journey for those who cannot cross into the next valley by the higher passes, on foot, or on horseback.

In these valleys there is generally a river (or '*Gave*,' as it is called in the language of the country), first a little rivulet or a leaping waterfall, then a roaring cataract, or a wide and turbulent stream, according to the formation of the valley through which it forces its way to the sea.

From the geographical position of the Pyrenees (42° N. latitude), the sun has much greater power than in Switzerland, the snow-level is consequently higher, and we find more fertile valleys, and mountains clothed, almost to their summits, with trees.[1] The green pastures high up the mountain sides, the luxuriant growth of the box tree, the rich foregrounds of ferns, the grandeur

---

[1] In Switzerland the peaks of the Alps may be said to *average* nearly 11,000 feet high, and the snow-level to be 7500 feet above the sea. In the Pyrenees there is no snow remaining below 9000 feet, and the highest peak, on the French side, is 11,000 feet. Thus it will be seen how little snow, comparatively, there is resting on the mountains of the Pyrenees.

of the pine forests, and the general warmth of colour of the vegetation in summer time, constituting the great beauty of Pyrenean scenery.

We miss, of course, the lakes, that are the charm of Switzerland, but there are the mountain torrents to explore to their sources; there is a perfect garden of wild flowers for the botanist;[1] plenty of work for the geologist; a little hunting, shooting, and fishing; and a wealth of mineral waters gushing from the rocks, which the Romans valued for the healing of their sick and which the French, in these latter days, have learned to utilise, and to convert into an attraction.

BORDEAUX.

Let us now take our little 'Moniteur' at its word, and start off to 'Les Eaux.'

Taking no heed of certain seductive advertisements, which are posted up all over Paris, concerning

> '*Voyages de plaisir aux Pyrénées.*'
> '*Billets de retour à prix réduits,*'

having nothing whatever to do with return tickets, we will take our places direct to Pau.

---

[1] See POSTSCRIPT, p. 241.

The night mail train to Bordeaux is one of the best appointed and most comfortable in France, leaving Paris in the evening, arriving at Bordeaux in the morning, and at Pau in the middle of the day. The journey can be easily broken by staying at Bordeaux, but for those of us who are hardy, and are anxious to waste neither time nor money on the road, it is better to go direct to Pau.

After an hour's halt at Bordeaux for breakfast, we are again on our way, and entering upon the quaint and picturesque district called ' LES LANDES,' so well depicted by M. Doré in these illustrations, the one on the opposite page being a perfect presentment of the scene from our carriage-windows.

This strange dull-looking tract of country, which stretches nearly the whole distance from Bordeaux to DAX, is planted with pine trees, divided by scanty patches of cultivation and acres of marshy ground, over which the mist hangs for miles.

It is difficult in the early morning to distinguish even the forms of the pine trees as we hurry past, and more difficult to persuade ourselves that there are human beings amongst the trees, and that they are tending sheep below them, where little pasture seems to grow.

Very quaint and strange these little figures appear in the distance, on their stilts (with a long pole to steady them, on the principle of a three-legged stool), propped up here and there like field scarecrows, which office they probably hold as well as that of shepherd. Here and there we see one start off on some errand, and it is curious to notice the pace at which they manage to get over the ground, taking tremendous strides with their stilts.

The inhabitants of 'Les Landes' are a hardy race,

THE LANDES

subject to great privations, especially the want of good water. They are accustomed from childhood to use these stilts, and to spend most of their lives in fieldwork, also in collecting resin from the pine trees, an industry from which they principally derive subsistence. The bark is sliced off, the trees are then tapped, and a vessel is placed below the incision in the trunk, into which the resin flows. The effect is very singular and striking when seen for the first time, especially in half light or when the day is breaking. As we pass through these plantations, we see numbers of pine trees taking quite a mutilated human appearance, their trunks cut and slashed about, giving up their life-blood, as it were, and dying fast one by one ; and the cork trees, also maimed, assuming most fantastic shapes, stretching out their numerous crippled limbs, as if appealing for commiseration. For miles in every direction we see nothing but the same broad plains covered with dismantled trees, and cannot help congratulating ourselves that the old diligence journey, with its weary, monotonous stages, is at last abolished.

Still the old system of travelling had its compensations, for we at least saw more of the country and the people, when after a long day with the broiling sun full upon us all the way from Bordeaux, we arrived towards evening at Dax, and saw the distant Pyrenees glowing in the setting sun ; having had leisure, during the numerous halts, to explore one or two of the curious old towns on the road.

The first of any importance which we pass is Dax, a fortified town on the river Adour, containing about 10,000 inhabitants 'enveloped in a cloud of steam.' Here there are remains of Roman baths, the ruins of an aqueduct, and several 'Établissements des Bains' for the curative waters.

THE LANDES.

The aspect of this place, when we last spent a day there, was quiet in the extreme, and there seemed little life or energy anywhere excepting amongst the bathers and in the manufactories near the river. The old ramparts, which form a sort of boulevard, or promenade round the town, are grass-grown and neglected; and were it not for the pleasant breezes that come from the mountains, and the distant views which we obtain from

DAX.

this spot, we should have found it dreary indeed. The one thing to do was to bathe in the almost scalding stream,[1] to walk, to breakfast, and to bathe again. Near the centre of the town there rose up a cloud of steam all day; on the ramparts in the afternoon the washerwomen brought their bundles to spread out on the walls, and the doctors their patients, to dry in the sun.

---

[1] 158° Fahrenheit.

DAX

The water of these baths, which has been in high repute ever since the time of the Romans, still attracts numerous invalids who have neither the strength nor the opportunity to visit the more fashionable watering-places of the Pyrenees. The water is disagreeable to the taste, and its density and colour are anything but inviting to the bather.

We said we found Dax dull in the 'season' and in fine weather; what it is like on a wet day the reader may judge from the letter of a friend, who, tired of watching the bathers at the 'Établissement,' 'rheumatic men and women sitting in the hot, black mud,' wrote home :—'A funeral procession passed us in the street, and I think I envied the occupant of the bier; he, at least, was leaving Dax, whereas I had to wait for the seven o'clock train!'

Twenty-five miles further on our journey, passing more cork trees, we come to the old historic town of Orthez (the ancient residence of the Princes of Béarn), with the ruins of the 'Château de Moncade.' This castle, standing in a commanding position above the town, is worthy of much more than the passing glance which a railway traveller generally gives it.

A stroll up to these ruins, and a peep under the old battlements and towers, the scene of terrible cruelties, in the 13th and 14th centuries, will carry us back in imagination to that age of picturesque chivalry of which Froissart speaks in his Chronicles—how the famous Gaston Phœbus, Count de Foix, held captive in these prison walls all the real, or fancied, enemies of his power; how the most deadly hand-to-hand encounters were fought, and re-fought, on the ivy-covered bridge below us, and how the victorious and cruel Gaston finally lost his own life in hunting the wild boar in the forests at the foot of these mountains, and was buried with pomp at Orthez.

'Memories of the middle ages' crowd upon us here, and there is so little of the stir and bustle of modern life, that it seems more natural and appropriate to picture it, as M. Doré has done, with groups of horsemen trooping up its avenues as of old.

There is no fear of being thought too progressive at Orthez. There is much more affinity with the twelfth than the nineteenth century. The old man who conducted us over the ruins and bowed low while he held

ORTHEZ.

his hat for a franc, was a thorough conservative, and hated steam.

On the road between Orthez and PAU (a distance of twenty-five miles, which used to take five hours by diligence), there is to be seen the ancient capital of Béarn, Lescar, and above the town, the ruins of a castle and of the church of *Notre Dame*, both of the tenth century, where it is said several of the princes of Béarn were buried. If we visit this spot from Pau, as we can easily do, we shall be amply repaid, not in finding tombs or many tenth-century relics, but from the complete idea we obtain when on the spot, as at Orthez, of the habits of warfare of these princes, their strategical skill and science, as displayed in the positions they chose for their castles and in their methods of building.

And it is from an eminence, not far from Lescar, that we who come from the north by the road, obtain our first good view of the beautiful fertile plain of Béarn, with its pretty villages, lying at the foot of the Pyrenees; the birth-place of many whose names are illustrious in French history, especially that of Henry IV., whose memory is identified with this district and with the Château of Pau, whose towers we see rising above the town.

CHAPTER II.

*PAU.*

THERE are some places in the Pyrenees that we shall best describe by comparing them for an instant to their prototypes in Switzerland.

Thus, in its situation, and in the circumstance of its being chosen as one of the starting-places for the mountains, Pau is the *Berne* of the Pyrenees. Like Berne, it has its history, its monuments, its peculiar customs, its interest as the capital of an industrious and thriving province, and, above all, the same glorious view of distant mountains.

From the terrace on the 'Place Royale' at Pau, one of the principal public walks near the centre of the town, a view of the western range is spread out before us, with the fertile Val d'Ossau in the middle distance, and the roaring 'Gave,' fed by glacier streams and swollen by torrents, immediately beneath, and we could not choose a more fitting or delightful spot for making our first acquaintance with the Pyrenees ; we are here, as it were, on the threshold of the sanctuary, at the very feet of the mountains, we feel their presence, and long to approach them. How shall we picture to the reader the scene on this fine summer afternoon in August ?

A luxuriant beauty of landscape—in the middle distance an undulating sea, soft in outline, varied in tint, half cloud, half mountain-top; rich pasture-land in the valleys, dotted here and there with white cottages and châteaux peeping through deep masses of foliage—a bright golden hue over the land, a purple mist amongst the hills, and a sweet wind coming from the south.

The Pic du Midi d'Ossau, which is the most prominent of the distant mountains, is thirty-three miles from us in a direct line, and is 9465 feet above the sea; but the outlines are so blended with the clouds, and the forms are altogether so indistinct, that we can form very little idea of their actual distance or height by the eye. We

VIEW FROM PAU.

shall approach them on our route to Eaux-Chaudes, by the broad valley immediately before us, but we must first see something of the town of PAU.

As we were jolted over the rough stony streets on our arrival yesterday, we had glimpses of a large and apparently thriving town, situated on an eminence 150 feet above the river, with a picturesque castle as its principal architectural feature, and a magnificent park of trees, extending for nearly a mile on high ground, by the banks of the Gave.

The population of Pau is about 30,000, increased in winter by a large number of foreigners, attracted both by the natural beauty of the situation and the reputation of the town as a mild and healthy winter place of residence. There are three or four important streets, of which the principal is the 'Rue de la Préfecture,' but the majority are narrow and irregularly built, and have no particular attractive features. There are, however, abundant signs of prosperity and wealth in the large new houses and hotels which have risen in every direction, and in the extent and almost Parisian variety of the wares in the shops; although in July and August the streets are half deserted, and the principal ones have almost as silent an aspect as a fashionable street in London out of the season.

It is only in the busy market-place, and in some of the nooks and corners of industry in the town, that we find much sign of commercial activity; and it is only on Sundays and fêtes, that many of the Béarnais are to be seen. Their costume is now so thoroughly modernised, that if it were not for the peculiar red and brown caps (berrets) worn by the men, and the striped handkerchiefs of the women, there would be little to distinguish them from the inhabitants of any other town in the south of France.

Pau, the ancient capital of the kingdom of Navarre and the chef-lieu[1] of the Basses-Pyrénées, occupies such an important place, not only in the estimation of the Béarnais themselves but in French history, that we must say a few words as to its origin.

The origin of the Château of Pau, and indeed of the

---

[1] A decree was passed on the 4th October, 1790, constituting the kingdom of Navarre, Béarn and the 'Pays Basques' one department, the 'chef-lieu' being fixed at Pau.

town itself, which was afterwards built round its walls, is indirectly owing to the Moors, who, crossing the Pyrenees from Spain, made such frequent sallies upon the Béarnais that their princes were compelled to fortify the strongest positions that commanded the plain. In self-defence the inhabitants of the Val d'Ossau gave permission to one of their princes to build a château on an eminence on the banks of the Adour, reserving to themselves certain rights and privileges of government.

On a plot of ground on the right bank of the Gave were planted three stakes (*palis*) to mark the boundaries, and on the spot where the centre one was planted the château was built, being called the '*Château de Pal*,' from thence 'Pau.'[1] A town soon began to spring up around its walls, and in the middle of the fourteenth century, under the

---

[1] On the arms of Pau, granted in 1482 (engraved at the end of this chapter), we see the three *palis* or stakes, over the middle of which there is a peacock with outspread tail, the whole surmounted by a crown and the cradle of Henri IV.

direction of Gaston Phœbus, Comte de Foix, strong fortifications were added, a church was built, markets and fairs were established, and various rights and privileges were conferred upon the inhabitants. It was thus that it became the capital of the kingdom of Navarre, being honoured with the title for the first time in a patent of Jean d'Albret and Queen Catherine his wife, in 1502; but what contributed afterwards to its growth and prosperity was probably its being the favourite resort of the kings of Navarre.

The climate of Pau, and its value to invalids as a place of winter residence, has, like that of other towns in the south of France, been a little over-rated, but statistically it is one of the most healthy,[1] and it has natural attractions almost unequalled.

Ever since 1814, when 5000 English soldiers, commanded by Lord Beresford, took forcible possession of Pau, it has been gradually growing into favour amongst English people, who form a little colony from October to May, or June, numbering more than three thousand, the completion of the railway from Paris bringing more visitors every year. The railway has its drawbacks, in converting what was once a snug little coterie of English people into a fashionable and expensive watering-place, where furnished houses in good situations are let for 300*l*. or 400*l*. for the winter season.

There is a resident English chaplain, an English club well supplied with books, and a good subscription library. There are golf and cricket clubs, a pack of hounds is kept by subscription, fishing, shooting, and plenty of gaiety during the winter in the way of balls and concerts, besides two theatres.

[1] See Dr. Taylor's 'Climate of Pau,' London : Churchill ; also Dr. Roth's Medical Notes on the Pyrenees, London : ·Baillière.

Fifty years ago, when the journey from England was much more expensive and tedious, the English residents numbered about forty, and it was possible to live here cheaply and well. It is true that the houses were inferior, that the streets were more badly paved than now, that there were few shops and not many of the luxuries of life, but a *furnished* house could then be obtained for 50*l.* a year.

From an original little pamphlet published at Avranches, we may gather one or two curious particulars of life at Pau at this period.

'Pau was a small and particularly foul town, of some 8000 to 9000 inhabitants, the residence of less than fifty English people, whose main attraction was economy. They took up their quarters often for years, and were not the birds of passage that now flock to it; they were content with houses of moderate size, moderately furnished, and there was a good deal of sociability and simplicity which have died a natural death.'

The climate seems to have been much the same as at present, but we are told that 'The sun in January used not to be thought so terrific as to require a calico covering to a man's hat, or a white umbrella over his head!' The Rue de la Préfecture was 'dirty, cold, and damp;' the Park was badly kept; and the 'well-like cold' of some of the dwelling-houses was thought worthy of record.[1]

It is interesting to learn also from the same authority that in those days the saddle or the sedan-chair, was the only means of locomotion; a mode of conveyance succeeded by a little one-horse vehicle, now uncommon,

---

[1] An expression, which we have heard residents make use of more than once, showing that invalids must be careful in the choice of their winter dwellings at Pau.

called satirically a 'vinaigrette,' a little box on wheels just large enough to hold one person, the driver running at the side. In those days good shooting was to be had; 'woodcocks, quails, and wild ducks were to be heard of in the neighbourhood, when at the present time there are a dozen chasseurs to every *pièce de gibier!*'

We hardly know whether to be amused at, or to regret, the change that has come over Pau. The town has greatly benefited by the influx of visitors, but 'society' has suffered. As an old resident expressed it to us, ' These thriving millionaires, these *rentiers*, oppress us; where they come from no one knows; they bring their families, their servants, their horses, and surround themselves with every luxury and comfort, and are to their poorer neighbours like a blight on the land.'

But, whether for good or evil, we have only to spend a few weeks here, to walk in the evening in the beautiful Park, to see the moonlight view from its terraces, to explore the environs, and enjoy the air even in the hot summer-time, to understand what brings so many of our countrymen hither. The remarkable stillness of the atmosphere (which in summer is seldom close, and in winter is delicious) is ascribed to the peculiar position of the town, sheltered on the north by the distant rising ground of the Landes, on the south and east by the mountains, and on the west by the Park itself, which presents a perfect wall of foliage against the wind. It is almost impossible to credit the fact, that in spite of the traditional stillness of the atmosphere at Pau, seventy-nine oak and beech trees were destroyed here in a storm, in one day.

To the passing visitor, the stillness of the air, the silence and somewhat neglected appearance of the town and its public walks, give it a mournful look. We see at once that Pau is not a very fashionable resort of the French, and are not long in perceiving (what we shall have plenty of evidence of by-and-by) that the natives care little or nothing for scenery, and continually turn their backs upon the mountains. The unrivalled site of this town has been wasted in later years by buildings of the manufactory type being erected so as to block out the best views; the Place itself is out of repair, grass-grown, and heaped up with rubbish and dead leaves; and if it were not for the fine modern hotels for English, French and American visitors, on the well-kept terrace facing the view, Pau would still appear behind-hand in the ways of civilisation.

But if the public walks and buildings have a generally neglected air; if the pavement of some of the streets is so much

THE PARK.

out of repair that 'au bout de cinq minutes vos pieds vous disent, d'une manière très intelligible, que vous êtes à deux cents lieues de Paris;' if the Park in autumn time is so strewn with dead leaves that its paths are obliterated—there is little sign of neglect or decay at the Château. Here, if anywhere, we should have hailed any marks of dilapidation, but everything is new and bright; for, as a half-satirical Frenchman expressed it, as nearly as we can remember his simile—'as the snow falls, obliterating landmarks, leaving all pure and white to view, so has an Imperial Providence, watching over Pau, covered these tottering ruins with fresh white stone, to the comfort of the custodian, and the despair of the antiquary.'

Approaching the Château by a street lined with

modern dwelling-houses and hotels, and entering the courtyard by a garden with smooth walks and trim beds of flowers, under a doorway or screen of newly-carved stone-work, it is evident that in a few years, busy hands will have so repaired, re-decorated, and improved (?)

the Castle, that its historic interest will be much diminished. Visitors are not permitted much time for regrets, for they are immediately placed *en queue* by polite attendants, and marched through a few of the apartments in less than half an hour.

Ascending a wide staircase which leads from the courtyard, we are conducted through a suite of rooms hung with old tapestries from the Gobelins and Brussels. The furniture is of the time of Henri IV., much of it collected and placed here by the late Louis Philippe: rich inlaid cabinets, marble tables, elaborately carved chairs and mantelpieces, medallions, jewels in cases, and various other works of art, set about in stiff and formal fashion. But in spite of the formality and stiffness (inseparable from state apartments on show), there are little nooks and corners in mullioned windows here and there, and certain signs of comfort and of having been *lived in*, that are charming in their suggestion of what this Château must once have been—in short, what, in England would be called, a 'perfect old home.'

In one apartment are some splendid porphyry vases, marble tables, &c., the gift of Bernadotte, King of Sweden; a collection for which a special permit should be obtained to examine at leisure.

Amongst the most interesting objects are the tapestries on the walls, delightful in their sobriety and repose of colour, wonderful in the blending of their delicate tints when contrasted with much of the furniture and gilding, and worthy of a much more careful inspection than visitors are allowed to give them. Ordinary visitors are hurried through all the rooms, and only allowed a short pause at what is considered the chief object of attraction, the cradle of Henri IV. made out of a large tortoise-shell, which is exhibited under a canopy

PAU

in one of the bed-rooms. The crowds of country-people that flock here on Sundays and holidays to see this relic, caring apparently for little else in the Château, attest the love and veneration that still exists for the memory of Henri IV.

We should not omit to mention the famous Tower of Montauzet, with its dungeons, on one side of the courtyard of the Castle, reminding us (not from its architecture, for this has little pretension) of another prison-house in the air, the tower of the Palazzo Vecchio at Florence. The Tower of Montauzet is nearly eighty feet in height, and the dungeons which are built into the thickness of its walls are about forty feet from the ground. The towers of the Château, and the exterior walls which almost overhang the river, are perhaps the most interesting parts of the building; the *Tour de la Monnoye*, where Margaret de Valois is said to have given an asylum to Calvin and other reformers, being the most ancient.

But we get very little idea of the outward aspect of the Château, and of the design of its founders as a building of defence, until we descend the steep bank, cross the bridge over the Gave, and obtain a view looking upwards, as in the last illustration. It is here that we see it in its picturesque character, and carry away a distinct remembrance both of the Château and of the town. Here let us remark in passing, how many cities owe their place in our recollection to some such distinctive (not necessarily historic, but prominent) architectural feature, some central point of interest and importance.

It is impossible to wander about Pau and the neighbourhood without being struck with the continual allusions to the memory of Henri IV. (as if he had reigned only yesterday), and at the same time, without noticing the absence of anything like a noble monument to his memory. On the terrace of the Place Royale, the Béarnais have erected a white marble statue to their beloved monarch; there are three bas-reliefs on the pedestal representing, first, the infancy of the prince, passed in the neighbouring mountains; second, his 'humanity' at the siege of Paris; and third, his bravery at the battle of Ivry. As a work of art it is poor and feeble, and in character and expression fails completely; we cannot realise in this image either the 'Solomon of peace' or the 'Cæsar of war,' nor trace any signs of that intrepidity of character, energy, or *bonhomie* of which we hear so much. M. Taine asks why they have made him look so sad, and suggests, perhaps with some reason, that he was weary of being praised by a faithful people!

An inscription written by a native poet (translated into modern French) runs thus:—

> 'Sais-tu quel est le Roi que t'offre cette image?
> Il fut grand, généreux, de son peuple l'ami;
> Idolâtré partout, à la ville, au village;
> Partout il fut pleuré . . . . J'y suis, c'est notre Henri!'

But however historians may differ in their estimate of the character of Henri IV., it is very certain that he held a high place in the affections of his people; his deeds are recorded in story and song, with the same simple affection that the English are accustomed to regard the memory of King Alfred; and we hear these songs so frequently in our travels, that it would hardly be doing justice to the loyalty of the poets of Béarn, if we did not give a translation in French of at least one of them.

The following, written in especial praise of '*noust Henri*,' 'our Henry,' as they love to call him, is a good example:—

> 'D'autres du grand Henri ont raconté la gloire
> Un poète fameux,[1] au temple de la mémoire,

---
[1] Voltaire.

Entre les meilleurs rois, a placé son beau nom ;
Sa vertu, sa valeur, ont partout grand renom.
Moi, je vais le montrer sortant de la coquille
Parmi ses Béarnais, au sein de sa famille.
Je dirai dans mes vers, comment ce roi nouveau
Fut soigné par nos mains en quittant son berceau.
O, France ! ce bon prince, objet de ton ivresse,
Ce prince à qui le peuple a gardé sa tendresse,
*Tu le dois au Béarn.*
\* \* \* \* \* \* \*
Prêtes nous la couleur et une style fleurie,
Allons, ne tarde pas ; c'est pour *notre* Henri.'

Is there not a charm about this song, a ring of true metal in its music, and a genuine expression of love and pride, especially in the last lines, that is rare in these days?

The Béarnais poems and ballads are exotic, and do not bear transplanting, or we should have been tempted to have given another extract ; we would suggest, however, to those who care for these things, that there is something quite foreign to the style of the majority of French writers—something, indeed, very like poetry—stored up or thrown aside, in the old song-books of the Béarnais, which our readers may discover for themselves, on high shelves, in the old book-shops at Pau, covered with the dust of time.

But we have come to see the mountains rather than the towns, and having taken our places in the diligence for to-morrow for Eaux-Chaudes, will go once more to the Place Royale, to see the view. The air is perfectly still on the terrace, but a few miles from us we can see tree-tops bending in the breeze, and the light fleecy clouds that surround the summits of the more distant mountains keep changing form as we watch them ; now descending into far-off valleys, nestling in their darkness for a while, like little snow fields, now dispersing suddenly, and casting soft shadows in their flight across the plain.

As we linger until sunset, the outlines of the mountains have gradually blended with fresh companies of dark clouds coming from the south, leaving the Pic du Midi d'Ossau alone above them shining in the sun, and the valley half hidden in a veil of mist. The aspect of the clouds is rather ominous for our journey, but of this we take little heed. The air, so pure, so soft, so still, seems to us perfection ; we can do nothing but marvel at the beauty of the scene, and thank from our hearts the princes of Béarn, for planting their *palis* by the Gave de Pau.

'Si vous \eniez à Laruns le dimanche, vous verriez danser les *branles*.'

## CHAPTER III.

### *VAL D'OSSAU—EAUX-CHAUDES.*

EARLY in the morning all the idlers at Pau are astir to see the start of the diligences for 'LES EAUX,' and at the 'bureau,' in the Rue de la Préfecture, we find plenty of activity and bustle.[1] There are several diligences, and they are all to be crowded to excess, and packed on the roof with merchandise to the last available inch of space. The travellers are, for the most part, French men and women with enormous boxes, bundles of warm wraps and walking-sticks, sun-shades of all colours, several little dogs, but no alpenstocks.

The author, whom we have taken for our 'compagnon de voyage,' remarks, respecting choosing places in a diligence, that it is better on all occasions to take the 'banquette,' or seat on the roof behind the driver; that it is true, if you fall, or the diligence is over-turned, you may get your head broken, but if not, you get the best view! It is no easy matter to scramble into this position, and sometimes more difficult to extricate yourself; and if (as is the case to-day) you find yourself wedged up against a pile of cheeses on one side, and baskets of live fowls in a state of semi-strangulation on the other, it is

---

\* A railway is in progress from Pau to Eaux-Bonnes—August, 1880.

questionable whether it is quite the position for the calm enjoyment of the scene en route.

The distance to Eaux-Bonnes is twenty-five miles, and to Eaux-Chaudes (to which we shall go first) twenty-seven, and the journey occupies six or seven hours; it is for the most part along a hot, dusty road, and the direction being due south, we have a steady tête à tête with the sun for the greater part of the day.

The diligences are neither better nor worse than is customary in France; they are easy and slow, dirty within, and gaily painted and mud-stained without. The five ill-conditioned little horses that rattle us over

the stony streets under the Castle walls, over the Gave, and out through the suburb of Jurançon, with a flourish, a jingle of bells and great promise of speed, soon subside into something like a walk and then go to sleep. The driver takes his breakfast (which he might have done before starting), smokes and receives visitors, until we have so many additions in the shape of peasant men and women hanging on to the steps and ledges of the vehicle that it groans under the weight. The heat soon becomes very great, and the dust, that travels with us, is almost intolerable; we roll on like a chariot of the sun riding on a cloud.

IN THE VAL D'OSSAU

After proceeding about fifteen miles in this fashion, it is a positive relief to arrive at the village of Louvie Juzon, where, on crossing a bridge over the Gave, the diligence is driven into a courtyard, the horses are taken out, and we are informed that we have an hour or more for '*restauration.*'

'Faites vous descendre à l'Hôtel des Pyrénées à Louvie, et demandez des rognons à la brochette et des truites fraîches,' are the pleasant instructions in a French guide-book, instructions that are carefully carried out by most of the passengers, but as we seem to have just breakfasted, we may do better by strolling out into the valley, or by the banks of the Gave, which is here a rapid and turbulent river, on the banks of which several companies of pigs are reposing in the sun.

In the first part of our route, we passed several little villages, and the private houses and country seats of some 'propriétaires'--through a pleasant, well-cultivated valley, watered by the river Neiss—and as we approached the town of Sévignac by a long ascent (where the Val d'Ossau was first entered), we gained occasional glimpses of the Pic du Midi.

The sides of these valleys are covered thickly with box-trees growing on the limestone rocks, and there is plenty of pasturage on the high ground. The lower part is almost always well cultivated and fruitful; we see corn and maize in abundance, and vines growing luxuriantly, trained upon maple and cherry trees. The women and children are at work in the fields, and the men tending sheep or collecting wood on the heights,

excepting when they are engaged in a more lucrative occupation. If we were asked what was the occupation of the inhabitants of these valleys, and were to answer from our own experience, we should say that in the summer it was *begging*. It is said that English visitors have completely demoralised the Valley of Chamounix, in Savoy, and that the curés are in despair; but whatever sins we may have committed in Switzerland, the French people have done worse, for the reason that the latter enjoy indiscriminate almsgiving, and we do not.

In the Pyrenees begging is decidedly encouraged;

what 'cold phlegmatic northerners' are apt to consider a nuisance, is a pleasure to a Frenchman, and nothing seems to make him happier than to be a dispenser of sous. The result in this valley is demoralising to an extent that would scarcely be credited excepting by eye-witnesses. As we drive along we see the peasantry leaving their work in the fields at the sound of approaching wheels, and crouching at the roadside in attitudes of pain and misery ; girls and boys leave their play to follow the carriages, and whine for ' *quelque chose ;*' crops are half gathered, and work of all kinds is neglected during the season of sous ; the cry is everywhere, 'Give, give,' for is it not the highway of the bountiful ? A girl of sixteen, well dressed and evidently well to do, comes up with a bouquet of wild flowers, which she has gathered at the roadside ; she asks ten sous for it (about the wages of a day's work), but she will take no less ; and on receiving the money will often ask for the bouquet back again, to sell to some one else. It is rather hard, as Tom Moore says,

' To be disturbed in romance by pecuniary views,
For whilst throwing their flowers they keep asking for sous.'

And this is not all, for those of the inhabitants who have not brought up their children to the liberal profession of begging, have invented another ingenious and profitable mode of life, that of turning the cascades in the neighbourhood into penny peep-shows, shutting them off, so that they can only be approached by a wicket gate, kept by one of themselves. But what can we say when the majority of visitors enjoy the giving ? we can only record the fact that wherever we go ' *Quelque chose, quelque chose pour l'amour de Dieu,*' is the chorus of the hills.

The most agreeable method of travelling in the

Pyrenees is undoubtedly to take a carriage with two horses, which may be hired for twenty-five francs a day, and retain it for the whole journey. Those who are not mountaineers have continually to retrace their steps to approach another point in the chain: thus when we have visited Eaux-Chaudes and Eaux-Bonnes, we must either return down the valley to reach Cauterets (a detour of about fifty miles, occupying two days), or pass over the Col de Torte on foot or on horseback.[1] The latter is rather steep, and fatiguing work, but Cauterets can thus be reached in one long day, and the views to be obtained on the bridle-road make it far preferable.

The expense of taking carriages in the Pyrenees is of course greater than going by diligence, but so much more is seen of the country, and it is altogether so much more enjoyable, when a pleasant party is made up, that it is worth while for English people to fraternise a little at Pau, or other starting-point, and join in taking a carriage, which easily accommodates four persons. Some of our pleasantest recollections of the Pyrenees are of parties made up accidentally, and continued through a tour of a month or six weeks—prolonged afterwards, as we heard in one instance, in a tour through life!

English people who have been accustomed to travel in Switzerland, and to 'have it all their own way,' as the saying is, soon discover that matters are not arranged here for their especial comfort or convenience; that in truth, their wants or wishes are very little considered in this country, and that there is a certain sense of isolation in their position, which tends to make them fraternise and travel together as much as possible. There are also other reasons for thus banding together as it were,

---

[1] A new but steep carriage-road is now open between Eaux-Bonnes and Arrens; to Argelès, but it is liable to be closed in the spring from snow.

VAL D'OSSAU

reasons which may develope themselves in the course of these travels.

But to continue our journey. Whilst we have halted at Louvie several carriages and diligences have passed, or put up at the inn, and out of perhaps a hundred travellers we have seen scarcely a dozen of our countrymen. Proceeding up the valley, still in a southerly direction, we pass near the ruins of the 'Castel Geloz,' an ancient château, which from its position must have been an important fortress in the times when each state held its own with a strong arm.

The valley is broad, but the mountains shut us in on both sides; they are cultivated to a considerable height, and we can see (with a glass) women making hay on the steep sides of the mountains, where there seems hardly foothold for an izard, and here and there can trace little white streaks that look like snow amongst the trees. These are the marble quarries for which the valley is famous, large quantities being excavated and sent to Paris and other towns in France every year.

In this part of the Val d'Ossau, in the little village of Bagés Beost, lives the French botanist, Gaston Sacage, whose collection of herbs and flowers of the Pyrenees is very curious and complete. Those who have time and are making collections, will do well to pay a visit to M. Sacage, who delights in showing and explaining his collection.

In two hours after leaving Louvie we arrive at Laruns, a town at the head of the valley, and the last in the Val d'Ossau. Here we leave the diligence (sending on our luggage), as the rest of the journey can easily be performed on foot. At this point we are in a complete *cul-de-sac*, from which we see no means of exit, excepting by retracing our steps. Immediately in front of us rises a bluff headland called the 'Mont de Gourzy,' and above it the prominent, and now to us familiar, Pic de Ger, but we can see neither the way to Eaux-Chaudes, nor Eaux-Bonnes.

Laruns is the 'chef-lieu' of the canton, a picturesque old town, with narrow streets and old gables; the centre of a large agricultural population, but much given in summer time to making money out of the crowds of pleasure-seekers who pass through every day. Its district reaches nearly to the frontier of Spain, and comprises within its limits the famous Pic du Midi. 'We are far from rich here, our mountain population pay no taxes and are rather unruly in the winter,' was a remark respecting Laruns which we did not understand, until we learnt that the 'unruly' part of the inhabitants consisted of izards (chamois), wolves, and bears![1]

On the day of our arrival Laruns is evidently *en fête*, there are more than a hundred people collected in the square and in the adjoining fields, dancing, singing, and enjoying themselves with the utmost freedom and content. In every direction we see peasants arriving, and there is a large contingent of the fashionable world who have come down from Eaux-Bonnes to see the fun.

The costume of some of the country people is very pretty and picturesque-looking, especially that of the women. The capulet, the characteristic, ordinarily white, head-dress of this valley, covering the head like the hood of a bournous, and reaching sometimes down to the waist (which so many artists have taken advantage of

---

[1] The *Hôtel des Touristes* at Laruns is a favourite resort for artists, not quite so popular, or so crowded, as the inn at Bettws in Wales, but possessing recommendations, both in accommodation and in the surrounding scenery, worth remembering by those who, seeking 'fresh fields and pastures new,' turn their steps towards the Pyrenees.

in their sketches in the Val d'Ossau), is especially captivating as a scarlet head-dress, covering a black bodice, and white full vest, open at the throat, sometimes adorned with a little gold cross tied with black velvet.

The men, with their embroidered cloth jackets, dark knee-breeches, scarlet vests, and gay sashes, wearing the 'berret' (a round flat cap made, indifferently, of red, white, blue, or brown cloth), with their canvas shoes tied with sandals, or with clogs turned up at the toes—are fitting partners for a rustic dance.

As the people flock in, old and young, the elder ones range themselves about the square, standing, or sitting on benches under quaint and dark old archways; the women with the spindle and distaff, the men with their pipes; groups appearing at odd-shaped windows overhead, men and children crowding upon carts, seated on horseback, or on raised seats, the whole forming a background for a scene which Wilkie would have delighted in.

It was no particular festival to-day (such as takes place on the 15th of August every year, when the whole valley takes part in it), but a sort of harvest-gathering and rejoicing, a 'rough and tumble,' with singing and dancing ad libitum. The instruments and music were simple enough, the former being principally a shepherd's pipe, and an instrument with two or three strings, struck with a stick, called a *tambourin*. The dances were taken to quick time, fifteen or twenty couples stood up and whirled away with all the energy of an Irish jig at a wake. There was none of that formality and ceremonious behaviour that we see sometimes so quaintly enforced in German villages and elsewhere—where the men scarcely speak to their partners, and directly each dance is over huddle together in one corner in a dark mass, like caged rats—but a hearty, jovial, devil-may-care spirit pervaded the company, young and old, that nothing could withstand.

There was certainly something catching in the music, simple though it seemed, that stirred the rustic performers to an amount of energy that was extraordinary (reminding us in its influence of the Spanish 'bolero,' that mysterious dance-music that acts as a charm on those who come within its influence), and which resulted in several heavy falls which we could not always see for the crowd, but which we were made aware of by a crashing sound, and by the shouts of laughter which greeted each downfall.

There were other sports and amusements at Laruns that day, but they were chiefly what we see at any fête in France, the favourite ones being 'roundabouts,' and shooting at effigies of popular characters; but the majority of the crowd in the afternoon, being clad in modern costume, the fête had more the appearance of a fair in the Faubourg St. Denis.

In the next sketch, at a shrine in the old church at Laruns, M. Doré has indicated some of the characteristic costume left amongst the people, but in a very few years, we venture to say, no such group will be found.

Let us here say a few words about the language and music of the people who inhabit these valleys.

In a little book on the 'Art of Travel,' which contains valuable hints to pedestrians on the mountains, the traveller is naïvely recommended, on all occasions, to enter into conversation with the wayfarers he meets, as one of the greatest sources of enjoyment and instruction. Presupposing that the traveller knows something, at least, of the language of the country through which he journeys, the writer says :—

'Your peasant companion will tell you about the old

ruin that crowns the height above his village, and some story connected with it not to be found in the chronicles. You may gather from his talk the records of local feeling; the certainty of a firm belief in an ancient superstition—a remnant, it may be, of heathen time, and

prevalent only in that neighbourhood—or he will relate all the details of some world-stirring event in which he or his father was an actor. From another you get an account of some grand natural phenomenon—a landslip, or an inundation—and his relation, with its natural earnestness and dramatic power, will have a charm that fixes your attention, and makes you feel sorry when the tale is ended.'

This is true enough, as our travelled readers well know, and few of us leave our native land without some knowledge of the language of the country we are going to visit. But in the Pyrenees this is not so easy, for the language spoken by the peasantry in the Val d'Ossau, and that of the Béarnais, differs so widely from French, that it is not until some time has been spent amongst the people that the ear becomes accustomed to the unusual sounds, and detects the similarities that really exist. Every day this distinction is becoming less marked, as railways bring the people more into contact, and in the neighbourhood of the large towns a language is growing into use partly French, partly Béarnais, partly Basque, and partly Spanish.

The Béarnais cling to their old customs with an almost childish faith, and believe in the purity of their language, and in its musical and expressive power. They say of it, perhaps with justice, that

> 'Comme la langue Espagnole et sa sœur l'Italienne,
> Seules la Béarnaise et la Languedocienne
>     Sont faites pour se mesurer,
> De prendre le haut vol qu'un autre s'avise
> Au Béarnais pour prier, pour aimer et bénir,
>     Rien ne se peut comparer.'

We will now give an example of one of their popular airs which have been handed down through several generations, and which are the sources of many 'modern' French songs. The following, which is both characteristic and curious, may have suggested to the minds of later composers, the familiar 'Jeannette and Jeannot,' or even the patriotic 'Partant pour la Syrie':

## ADIÜ LA BÈRE MARGOUTOU.

## ADIEU LA BELLE MARGOTON.

*Béarnais.*

Adiü la Bère Margoutou !
Tu bas perdé toun serbidou !
   Jou baü party,
   Per lou Rey serby.
Maüdite sie la guerre !
   Dens sas amous
   D'aüta malurous
N'ou'n badou sus la terre !

Dens moun estat, biby countén,
Nou mancabi d'or, ni d'argén,
   Dé bèts chibaüs,
   Dé richés cabaüs ;
Ségu dé ta tendresse . . .
   Tout qu'ey pergut !
   Lou sort m'ey cadut !
Moun Diü, quine tristesse !

Jou bé't aymi, bé't aymérèy,
Margoutou, tan qué jou biürèy ;
   Si pouch quita
   Berleü haü tourna,
Et pendén la campagne,
   Si y a papè,
   You t'escriürè
Deü houns dé l'Allemagne.

Qu'aüras recoumandatious,
Et noubelles dé mas amous ;
   Toun noum au cap
   Et Pirre sinnat,
En lettres d'or l'addresse.
   Y aura dessus :
   'Taüs mouts sien renduts
A ma bère mestresse.'

Si'm mori, bère Margoutou,
Aco sera deü maü, d'amou,
   You'n soy countén ;
   Et per testamén,
Bouy esta houtat en terre,
   Et sus lou clot,
   Qué legen, Margot :
*Ci-git moun amic Pierre.*

*Translation.*

Adieu la belle Margoton !
Tu vas perdre ton serviteur !
   Je vais partir,
   Pour servir le roi.
Maudite soit la guerre !
   Dans ses amours
   D'aussi malheureux
Il n'en naquit sur la terre.

Dans mon état je vivais content,
Je ne manquais ni d'or ni d'argent,
   De beaux chevaux,
   De riches réserves ;
Assuré de ta tendresse.
   Tout est perdu !
   Le sort m'en est échu !
Mon Dieu, quelle tristesse !

Moi je t'aime, je t'aimerai.
Margoton, tant que je vivrai.
   Si je puis quitter
   Bientôt je vais revenir,
Et, pendant la campagne,
   S'il y a du papier,
   Je t'écrirai
Du fond de l'Allemagne.

Tu auras des compliments
Et des nouvelles de mes amours ;
   Ton nom en tête
   Et Pierre signé,
En lettres d'or l'adresse.
   Il y aura dessus :
   ' Que ces mots soient remis
A ma belle maîtresse.'

Si je meurs, belle Margoton,
Ce sera du mal d'amour,
   J'en suis content ;
   Et par testament,
Je veux être mis en terre,
   Et sur la fosse
   Qu'on lise, Margot,
*Ci-git mon ami Pierre.*

We were about to add from our own experience, that some of the sounds in the Béarnais dialect, and the words of their songs in the original patois, seem harsh and discordant after Parisian French, and that, however well adapted for musical expression, there were certain syllables that grated upon our northern ears; but M. Taine here takes us by the button-hole, and tells us the following little anecdote, apropos. Coming down a mountain one day with a party, in the Pyrenees, they heard voices behind them amongst the trees; doubtful as to who might be following, they listened attentively, and were soon enlightened.

'Nous entendons,' he says, 'un gloussement aigre, comme d'une poule étranglée, et nous reconnaissons la langue anglaise!'

Leaving Laruns—parting with most of our companions, for nearly every one goes to Eaux-Bonnes—we traverse an open space where the marks of the overflow of the torrent (which we cross by a fine stone bridge) and the débris brought down by storms, are everywhere apparent, and we come into quite a corner at the end of the valley.

How, in old times, visitors to 'Les Eaux' ever managed to scramble up the precipitous sides of the mountain before us, and by what means invalids were carried thither for the benefit of the waters, seems at first sight extraordinary; but when we examine the head of the valley more closely we can understand how the mountaineers of those days, following, by habit or instinct, the courses of the streams that come down on either side, made their way by more circuitous routes. Thanks, however, to the enterprise of M. Boura, a native engineer, Eaux-Bonnes is now approached by a fine broad road cut in the limestone rock by a series of easy zigzags, which command fine views down the valley.

CHAP. III.   VAL D'OSSAU.   47

At a short distance after commencing the ascent, the road divides and we turn to the right, through a wild and narrow gorge that leads to Eaux-Chaudes. Through the dark and gloomy portals we slowly ascend

ROUTE TO EAUX-CHAUDES.

by a smooth and admirably constructed road, which was completed in 1847. In many places it has been made by blasting rock on both sides, making an opening just wide enough for the road, and for the torrent, which here confined between two walls comes down with great velocity. At one point the road has had to be built up against the side of the rock like a bridge, to allow a torrent which falls from a height of several hundred feet, to pass *under* it and so join the Gave, the main stream that runs into the valley, called here the 'Gave de Gabas.'

Soon after passing this bridge the valley opens out, as we see in the illustration. The sides of the mountains, which are upwards of 2000 feet high, are covered with trees, excepting where torrents have laid them bare, and convulsions of nature, or the work of man, have detached huge masses of limestone into the Gave. The valley, although wider and more open on the high ground, is steep near the road, for the mountains almost meet at their base, and all the way to Eaux-Chaudes, a distance of about three miles, there is little to be seen besides the road and the Gave, and the mountain sides. About an hour after leaving Laruns we see before us a little smoke or steam curling up in the still air, which we first take to be a woodman's fire, but which in reality rises from Eaux-Chaudes.

In a little corner, on the right bank of the Gave, where the mountain sides are almost perpendicular on the east, or right bank, and the river roars below on the west, at a point where from a mixed bed of granite and limestone the hot sulphureous springs burst forth, we find EAUX-CHAUDES, consisting of a little street of poorly built houses, two or three hotels, and a handsome marble 'Établissement des Bains.' The latter is built on a platform almost overhanging the torrent; it has a large hall or pump-room, and promenade, fitted up with seats and stalls for the sale of all kinds of knicknacks; there are a number of private baths, and accommodation for

ROUTE TO EAUX-CHAUDES.

patients suffering from rheumatism and other ailments, who are under the care of a resident physician. There are people sitting in a little garden trimly laid out, in front of the 'Établissement,' and others walking about with tumblers, going through a course of the waters; following the routine of the last three hundred years, since the time when the bishop of Oléron, Chancellor of Béarn and Foix, first established here a ' maison d'habitation,' by order of Henry of Navarre.

The situation of Eaux-Chaudes is so confined that every square yard of space has had to be built upon and utilised, and at the side of one of the hotels a little terrace or promenade has been constructed almost over the Gave. On this the 'administration' have planted trees and placed seats, and it is between this spot and the Établissement that the valetudinarian, who is not robust enough to clamber up the mountains, has to alternate and to spend his days, varied only by a drive up the valley to Gabas, or down by the route we have just come.

If there is a gloomy and deserted appearance about Eaux-Chaudes, even on a fine summer's afternoon, when the sun, which only shines upon the place for a few hours, is lighting up the trees above our heads with that peculiar and brilliant golden green that tinges orange groves in the setting sun; when the cattle are returning from the high pastures and the tinkle of bells is heard in every direction, and the visitors, perhaps a hundred, are moving about in their confined area—what must it be like when the clouds come down, (as they do nearly every other day,) and completely shut the inhabitants off from all view, either of the sky, or of the route up and down the valley, and when the roar of the wind is added to that of the torrent?

ENVIRONS OF EAUX-CHAUDES.

It has been frequently urged in guide-books that it is better for travellers to take up their quarters here, than at Eaux-Bonnes, but after repeated visits to both we decidedly recommend the latter, and we have seldom met with people who were not of the same mind. Eaux-Chaudes is cheaper, and is not overwhelmed with the 'haut monde;' it is also well placed for excursions on the high Alps, but *it is situated in a gloomy thorough draught*.

The environs are wild and beautiful in the extreme, and it is to explore these at leisure, to sketch the valley from different points, to examine the extraordinary stratifications of granite and limestone, to mark the traces of extinct glaciers, to collect fossils or wild-flowers, to fish in the Gave, or to hunt the izard, (each one according to his taste) that this valley recommends itself for a lengthened visit.

The finest excursion is up the valley, southwards, past Gabas, a little hamlet five miles from Eaux-Chaudes, to the 'Plateau de Bioux Artiques,' three miles farther, from which we obtain a magnificent view of the Pic du Midi d'Ossau, a mountain we had almost forgotten, so shut in have we been since leaving Laruns. There is a good carriage road to Gabas, and the valley, notwithstanding its height, and its comparatively sterile aspect, is one of the most varied and beautiful in the Pyrenees.

As the valley opens out again we see the sides of the mountains covered with pastures and wild-flowers. There are beech and oak trees sheltering patches of cultivated ground, cattle feeding on the slopes, and women working in the fields, as in the Val d'Ossau; many of the more distant granite rocks are covered with dark firs, mingling with the lighter foliage of the beech,

CHAP. III.     EAUX-CHAUDES.     53

oak and birch ; and, lower in the valley, the box-tree hides the chasms and cascades with its luxuriant growth.

Gabas itself is a lonely little hamlet, (3657 feet,) the last on the French side of the Pyrenees, a halting-place for travellers, and for the carriers who pass here on their way into Spain. Sometimes we may see, resting under the trees, a party of Spanish muleteers, and in the fine summer weather, many travellers coming over from Panticosa on mules, to avoid the circuitous and expensive route by St. Sebastian. Spanish ladies are

ABOVE GABAS.

carried in chairs, or on mule-back, propped up by cushions, travelling most comfortably in this fashion, accompanied by their children and servants ; the journey from Panticosa to Eaux-Chaudes being thus accomplished in one day.

At Gabas the road divides, the path to the left leading to Panticosa, that to the right to the 'Plateau de Bioux Artiques,' where, in an hour and a half after leaving

Gabas, we obtain the view of the Pic du Midi, which it is said is 'worth coming all the way from Paris to see.' The path leading up to this plateau is lined with fir-trees, and on every side there are marks of the ravages of storms, that sweep down this valley with terrible force. In some places the mountain sides have been cleared of the timber by fire, or the trees have been felled for use, and the lopped trunks rolled into the torrent below, to float down the Gave into the plain.

In three hours more we could reach the base of the Pic du Midi itself, but the view is scarcely as fine as from the plateau, where its 'forked' ridge is seen to the best advantage.

The stern, cold appearance of this part of the valley, with its grey rocks and forests of pines, is relieved by the beautiful purple iris, that sheds a bloom over the lower slopes of grass, and by occasional patches of snow in the crevices of the rocks.

Here we were naturally anxious to ascertain something about the bears from which the Val d'Ossau takes its name, but could ascertain very little; the people are ready to get up an expedition to hunt them, but our guide, who was born in this valley, confessed that he had never seen a bear.

Returning in the evening to Eaux-Chaudes, some workmen who are busy repairing a stone bridge, are leaving their work and crowding into the town. There are, perhaps, thirty of them, masons and labourers from the valley, and as they go they sing and shout at the top of their voices, awakening strange echoes in the valley with their songs. What they sing, and how they can find amusement or pleasure, in such uncouth sounds, especially, when assembled on the terrace in the evening they favour us with the whole of their repertoire, was a

EVENING, NEAR GADAS.

matter for wonderment, and in truth we often wished them away. But one becomes accustomed to everything, and in a few days we looked upon these evening concerts as part of the life at 'Les Eaux.' The chorus of one song, often repeated, ran thus:—

> 'Les tailleurs de pierre
> Sont de bons enfants ;
> Ils ne mangent guère,
> Mais ils boivent longtemps !'

      \*    \*    \*

There was neither rhyme, nor melody, in most of these songs, and some seemed rather 'broad,' to unaccustomed ears, but they were vigorous and characteristic, free, gallic, and hearty ; better than the songs of the Boulevards.

Later in the evening, the services of a blind fiddler (whose portrait M. Doré has drawn for us) being retained, rustic dances are improvised. Several young men and girls stand up, and at first the dance is very grave and measured, like a Louis Treize minuet; then a lively step, the famous 'saut basque,' and at last the 'branle,' a veritable romp in which all take part, such as we saw at Laruns in the valley.

We had very comfortable quarters at the Hôtel de France, at Eaux-Chaudes, but did not spend much time within doors in fine weather ; and life here was, we need hardly say, very uneventful.

Some years ago on our way down this valley, we stopped to dine at this hotel ; we had come over the mountains by the Col de Gourzy and were without luggage and almost without purse, having (as Englishmen often do) left our effects at Eaux-Bonnes; and after paying for our dinner, our united resources amounted to a franc and a half. As ill luck would have it, a report came in that one of the workmen on the road had been seriously injured by the fall of some rocks, and a subscription was at once set on foot for his family. A paper was made out and handed to all at the table, many giving ten, or at the least, five or six francs each. The two Englishmen were left to the last, and a handsome gift was evidently expected. The position was not a little embarrassing, for the case was really a hard one, and the liberality of the company undoubted. However, there was nothing for it but to contribute our mite, and pocket the odium. The subscription-list was handed to a lady at the head of the table, who read out to the assembled company, the donors' names and the amounts subscribed. When it came to our turn, and 'MM. ——, 1 fr. 50 c.' was announced, every countenance fell, traditional French politeness gave way under the strain, and the liberality of 'les Anglais' (who were not supposed to understand what was said) was made the subject of the freest and most open comment we ever experienced in a mixed assembly. 'Oh mon Dieu, ces misérables! soixante quinze par personne!' 'Trois pauvres petits enfants—cinquante centimes, chaque!' It got into the papers afterwards, but we were out of harm's way, up amongst the mountains again, fitter company for bears!

This event was a 'godsend' at Eaux-Chaudes, for the visitor's, or the invalid's day, even in the finest weather, is monotonous enough. There is the usual round of bathing, drinking the waters, reading old newspapers,

COL DE GOURZY; AFTER A STORM

promenading, dining, and perhaps dancing a little in the evening, that we shall meet with continually in our journeys through the Pyrenees; but so little love for the mountains or interest in the beauties of Nature, do we find amongst the *habitués* of the place (some of whom have come every season for years), that it is wonderful how such an existence can be endured.

For ourselves we can only say that most of the days at Eaux-Chaudes were (to use a paradox) generally spent out of it. So shut in is Eaux-Chaudes by huge mountain walls, that it is a positive relief to go somewhere every day, if only as far as the Col de Gourzy, to catch a glimpse of distant peaks, and breathe the higher air.

Then on summer nights, when the mountains seem to close over us, and every sound is echoed with wonderful distinctness through the valley; when the murmuring of the Gave, the wind in the trees, the tinkle of bells, the cries of shepherds, and the bleating of flocks in front of our open windows, continue almost incessantly through the night, we have sometimes wished for a little more peace; and could sympathise with an imaginative Parisian who (transported in a few hours from his beloved Boulevards, to a shelf of granite two thousand feet above the sea) used to dream that he was dwelling on the edge of some precipitous cliff, with the stars above him, and the sea roaring at his feet.

'Promenade Horizontale.'

## CHAPTER IV.

### *EAUX-BONNES.*

THE distance from Eaux-Chaudes to Eaux-Bonnes by the road, is not more than five miles, and there is constant communication by carriages and diligences during the summer months; but on the path over the Col de Gourzy, the mountain that separates us from Eaux-Bonnes (6000 feet high), we obtain such splendid views, that it is the route to be recommended for riding or walking, although rather rough and steep, and taking at least four hours.

By the high road we return down the valley, nearly to Laruns, and then, turning southwards again, commence ascending the fine road that we mentioned in the last chapter. The way is steep and slow for horses, but if we get out and cut off the zigzags by scrambling up the narrow paths, or make a détour to see the 'Grotto of Bears,' or the once famous 'Belvedere Fanny,' we shall yet arrive at our destination long before the carriages.

As we keep ascending, the view of the valley becomes more beautiful and forms a fresh picture at almost every turn of the road, and our attention is so entirely fixed upon what is passing below, where we can just distinguish the figures of the peasantry arriving at, and leaving Laruns, that we have scarcely once looked upwards. What is it that we see immediately overhead? What are those little specks of red and white moving amongst the trees far above us ? They are the picquets, or outposts, of a 'high civilisation' to which we must now introduce the reader.

A few more turns in the ascent, and we can distinguish people riding or walking, first by twos and threes, then a crowd. Where do they come from ? We can see no sign of a town—nothing but the valley below

and a few yards of the road, now neatly swept and railed off like the drive in a private park. We are no longer in the country ; we are 'en promenade.' 'Je comptais trouver ici la campagne,' writes M. Taine, 'je rencontre une rue de Paris, et les promenades du Bois de Boulogne !' We were of course somewhat prepared for this, but not altogether for the extraordinary sight that burst upon us on turning the road once more, and coming suddenly upon Eaux-Bonnes.

Here in a cleft in the mountain-side, overshadowed and overhung by rocks and trees, is a fashionable little hotel-village, consisting of about thirty houses and hotels, and giving accommodation in the season to six or eight hundred people.

On an area of not much more than half an acre, the ingenious founders of this little town have managed to lay out a 'Place' with trees and fountains, and two rows of hotels and pensions on either side, forming what is called the Grande Rue. At the upper end, built into the rock, is the Thermal Establishment, with its courtyards and promenades for bathers, and near it, a little church. One or two streets lead out wherever a nook and cranny could be found for them. One is called the Rue des Cascades, and another, which resembles nothing so much in shape as a narrow slice cut out of a cake, is dignified with the name of Rue de Cauterets.

In whichever direction we turn there are houses built into, and often forming part of, the mountain, resting on ledges of rock, like the eyries; but so cleverly contrived is the arrangement of the place, so admirably has space been economised, that there is a feeling of freedom about it, quite inconsistent with living in a bird's-nest.

Thus with the mountains several thousand feet above our heads, and the Val d'Ossau stretching away for many miles at our feet, with rocks overhanging and tree-tops waving *below*, through which we can see the blue sky—with scarcely a foot of level ground anywhere (save the 'Promenade Horizontale,' of which we shall speak presently), with cascades and waterfalls almost at our windows, we find ourselves as comfortably and luxuriously housed as in any modern city.

As we drive up to the door of the Hôtel de France, we are blocked several times by a crowd on foot and on horseback; and in the Jardin Anglais, or on the 'Place,' in front of the hotels, there are at least a hundred and fifty people making holiday after the manner of their respective nations.

THE PIC DE GER.

Looking down upon the Place from our hotel window on this bright sunny afternoon, it is the gayest scene imaginable; and we scarcely know which to admire most, the costumes of the fair riders who about this hour (five P.M.) come flocking in, dressed in white riding-habits and scarlet hats; or their cavaliers in buff and green, like members of the 'Ancient Order of Foresters;' or their dandy guides, in embroidered Spanish costumes, silk sashes, and white stockings; or the gay trappings of their thin steeds; or the motley group that stand about to see the arrivals. This last comprises every Parisian *fantaisie* and extravagance in attire, brought up here in those huge boxes, that are the *bêtes noires* of all occupants of the diligence banquette—bright plumage for the inhabitants of our little nest, strange importation into the Vale of Bears!

The noise and bustle in the squares (instruments playing more discordant music than any Italian organs), the squeaks and rattles of juvenile civilisation, the chattering of their *bonnes*, the incessant ringing of bells, the shouts and cracking of whips, the voices of different nations—all confined within a limited space, and echoed back from the surrounding rocks, can scarcely be conceived. But everything is sunshine, politeness, and apparent gaiety, 'la vie aux eaux;' a scene thoroughly unique, curious, and grotesque—'grotesque qu'un peu d'eau chaude ait transporté dans ses fondrières la cuisine et la civilisation!'

The cuisine is well provided, as we shall find presently if we join the company who are now assembling in the handsome salle à manger of the hotel for the table d'hôte. They consist principally of French people; a few Spaniards, and fewer English, Americans, Germans, and Russians. The English are in a decided minority at Eaux-Bonnes, as elsewhere in the Pyrenees, and are, to tell the truth, not too popular. The ruddy English face does not command universal sympathy and attention here, as in Switzerland, even amongst the class most open to impressions—waiters, servants, and guides. For once (and perhaps it is good for us) we do not have everything our own way.

The table is laid for about eighty people, and fifty or sixty or seventy sit down. The French—the habitués ('pensionnaires')—occupy one end, nearest the head of the table. They are elegantly dressed, courteous, and well bred, evidently belonging to the upper classes of society; in fact, were we to mention the names of some assembled to-day, they would be familiar in the diplomatic and literary circles of several European capitals. That M. Fould is here, is a fact considered worthy of large type in the local papers, with the intelligence that 'chaque matin il vient en calèche comme un simple mortel, prend son bain, déjeune et s'en retournerait à la fin de la saison avec une nouvelle jeunesse!' Next to the French sit the Spaniards, who are also well dressed but far less talkative; then there is a hiatus, with the English, Americans, Germans, Russians, and 'casuals' at the bottom.

As we are a holiday party, and have brought all the latest Parisian fashions, our toilettes are not only handsome, but there is an air of distinction about the company which one rarely sees at an hotel in France, excepting in the capital; a contrast to some dreary tables d'hôte in the provinces, which are generally composed of travelling English, and French *commis-voyageurs*.

We are merry and noisy, we might almost say uproarious, in spite of nationalities, and the gaps in our ranks. A wonderful clamour of plates and dishes, snatches of conversation, lively sallies across the table, disjointed accounts of 'ascensions' more or less exciting according to the style of the narrator, a rather peculiar manner of eating, and an unparalleled consumption of vin ordinaire, is roughly, what is passing at the further end of the table. The Spaniards who occupy the centre,

F

with an aristocratic solidity peculiarly their own, make great havoc with the viands, and lose no time in conversation. They have come with their families to spend the hot months at Eaux-Bonnes and to drink the waters ; and prove, as far as our experience goes, much more pleasant and genial travelling companions when away from their own country.

We said that they did not converse much, but we must make exception in favour of one delightful little man, about whom the reader will pardon us for saying a few words, because he is a type of the Spanish butterfly that we shall often meet in our journey through the Pyrenees. It has been our lot to meet him in many lands, but, wherever met, always devoting himself to the contemplation of female beauty. Whether at Homburg or Baden, at Paris or Biarritz, or on the banks of Lake Leman (where we have seen him the pride and ornament of the 'Hotel of the Beautiful Shore'), superbly dressed, an accomplished linguist, a perfect musician, skilled at croquet, equally at home with Russian countesses, brewers' daughters, and American maidens—amusing, volatile, rich, and happy. He was one of those birds of rare plumage and mysterious origin that flutter for a time round the court of Madrid,—basking in the sunshine of present prosperity. A little while (even whilst we write, the clouds seem gathering again) and the crash must come, when the dust will be dashed from these butterflies' wings, and Baden and Luchon will know them no more. Here, at Eaux-Bonnes, by art or accident, he is seated, as usual, opposite to the prettiest girl at the table, and is making the most of his opportunity. He has no time to lose, for when the cold winds come, he will be off with the swallows to the south of Spain.

Our own end of the table is, we fear, scarcely so brilliant in appearance, or so fluent in French, nevertheless we are sociable enough. There are grave 'patres familiarum' who are here with their families, for the benefit of the waters; one or two members of the Alpine Club, who have 'come down' to Eaux-Bonnes[1] for a change, and entertain us with accounts of their guides, who seem to be a peculiarly lazy race; London physicians, taking a brief but vigorous holiday, forgetting appointments, breathing the free air of unpunctuality and revelling in a suit of tweed; a few ordinary tourists, and the two English ladies that are to be met with almost everywhere in Europe, travelling together. We had almost forgotten an American gentleman at the lower end of the table, who entertained us with his views upon sovereignty, explaining to a Russian next to him, that reigning, having lost all sanctity and prestige, had become 'one of the open professions;' and we had also nearly omitted to mention that, to add to the concert of voices, we were favoured during dinner with the most discordant sounds. A blind fiddler (our old enemy from Eaux-Chaudes) was led into the room, and obliged us with several excruciating morceaux.

It is now past seven o'clock, and most of our party have dispersed, the majority betaking themselves to the Jardin Anglais or to the 'Promenade Horizontale.' This walk, which we will call by the less prosaic title of the Lady's Mile, is a perfectly level and smooth promenade cut round the mountain side for nearly half a mile, and is the only level ground at Eaux-Bonnes. It is lined for some distance with little shops and stalls, where bright-coloured Spanish wools, trinkets, and toys are

---

[1] Less enterprising mountaineers consider that they have already come *up* to it!

sold, where bagatelle and *tir au pistolet*, roundabouts and peep-shows—all the 'fun of the fair' in fact, is set going for the amusement of idle Eaux-Bonnes. From the seats placed at intervals on this wonderful platform the views down the valley, northwards, are most beautiful, with the little villages like specks in the distance, and the town of Laruns spread out in the shape of a cross at our feet.

As soon as it is dark the stalls and little wooden shops are lighted up, and promenading continues until about nine o'clock. The evenings are cold by contrast —colder than anything we have yet experienced, and many retire to the hotels, or to a little 'café chantant' in a hole cut in the rock, or to see a Parisian conjuror. There is a Cabinet de Lecture, but there are not many readers, and a Casino, which is also rather thinly attended.

The little square in front of the hotels is full of people, who assemble in the evening with their families, to hear a band that we have already heard too often: there are a great many guides and couriers sauntering about, and considerable interest seems to be taken in an expedition to hunt the izard, which is to take place to-morrow.

But it is not until later in the night, when Eaux-Bonnes has gone to sleep, that we can appreciate the beauty of our mountain home, when the universal hubbub has subsided, and we can hear for the first time the sound of innumerable cascades, and the rustle of invisible tree-tops in the evening breeze; when the smoke from this great seething kitchen has ceased to curl up the rocks, revealing the stars that shine with a brightness never seen in the plains.

The weather seemed so favourable for seeing the mountains, that we determined to make our first ex-

*'The sultry summer day is done,
The western hills have hid the sun,

But mountain peaks still rising higher,
Retain reflection of his fire.'

cursion the very next day, intending, if possible, to ascend the Pic de Ger, the extraordinary conical mountain that we see in the illustration at page 63. With some difficulty, and at a high rate of pay, we had managed to obtain guides who would walk, and carry our provisions without extra porters to help them. Our

chief guide prophesied a clear day for the excursion (which did not strike us as exhibiting much wisdom or foresight), adding that 'il faut profiter du temps' in this treacherous Val d'Ossau, for that 'there was no knowing what might happen.'

What did happen our readers may judge from the next illustration, and to what an unwelcome sound we awoke next morning--the sound of pattering of feet and the pattering of rain. Water everywhere—clouds resting upon the housetops, shutting off all view beyond our little square, and a brave army of invalids under umbrellas, taking the waters.

Let us follow them to the 'Établissement,' that we can just see through the rain, at the end of the street. It is a plain building of no architectural pretensions, which was once considered large, but is now quite inadequate to the requirements of Eaux-Bonnes in the height of the season. Visitors complain loudly of want of accommodation, especially in bad weather, when they have to stand upon the damp ground to wait their turn to drink the waters, and often find it difficult to get baths at the prescribed hours. There are seven sulphureous springs at Eaux-Bonnes; the principal are La Source Vieille, 88° (from which they drink), La Source Nouvelle, 86°, and La Source de la Douche, 91° Fahrenheit.

Whether it be good for any one, especially for those affected with pulmonary complaints (these waters being prescribed in the early stages of consumption), to stand about here in the damp, on these cold wet mornings, we will not stay to inquire, regretting only with our French friend that 'l'économie de l'administration suppose qu'il faisait toujours beaux temps,' and does not provide for bad weather.

It is said that the comfort of bathers is now better cared for at Eaux-Bonnes, under the direction of Dr. Pietra, the resident physician and Government Inspector; but both here and elsewhere in the Pyrenees, we shall find the Thermal Establishments far inferior in their interior arrangements and management, to those in other parts of the Continent.

'Il faut supporter la pluie et la musique aux Eaux-Bonnes!'

About ten o'clock we return to breakfast, and for an hour afterwards there is nothing to do on this wet morning but to listen to the German band, who, prisoners like ourselves, take up their position in the salon of the principal hotel, and discourse most eloquent music.

At eleven, it being a Saint's Day, and the weather slightly clearing, there is a general movement to the chapel, which is often too small for the wants of visitors; many of whom have come from the village of Aas.

'Cette église,' says Taine, 'est une boîte ronde, en pierres et en plâtre, faite pour cinquante personnes, où l'on en met deux cents. Chaque demi-heure entre et sort un flot de fidèles. Des prêtres malades abondent, et disent des messes autant qu'il en faut : tout souffre aux Eaux-Bonnes du défaut d'espace, et on fait queue pour prier comme pour boire.'

Soon after noon, the cloud that has so completely encompassed us, lifts a little, and in half an hour has disappeared altogether. The streets and walks quickly dry up, and are again crowded with people. The day is too far advanced, and the weather too uncertain to make any long excursions, so that we may as well employ our time in looking about us a little, and observing a few of the peculiarities of 'Les Eaux.'

Everything, we notice, seems adapted for a long stay; people who come here are evidently expected to remain for the season, and visitors who wish to see the chief places of interest and hurry off again, meet with various opposing forces. If you wish to take a bath, you have to pay an entrance fee of several francs, and are expected to subscribe for a 'course,' available for the season; at the Casino and reading-rooms the system is the same, and hotel prices are exorbitant by the day, but moderate by the week. To get a good mount you must hire your steed by the week or month, and take him, for better or for worse, for the season; and there are cascades to be viewed on the same principle.

We are all kept in good order here, everything is *en règle* and *à la règle*, and if we stay a whole season, we need not be at a loss how to get through the days. It is all arranged for us; there is the particular promenade for the early morning facing the east, the exact spot where you are to walk (and no farther) between the time of taking each glass of water, the after-breakfast cascade, the noon siesta, the ride at three, another cascade and more water, or a bath, at four, promenade at five, dinner at six, 'promenade horizontale' until eight, then the Casino,[1] balls, 'société' écarté, or a moonlight walk—and then, decidedly early to bed.

There is no real difficulty in thus getting through the days, but, perhaps, after a few weeks, we may get a

---

[1] A favourite place of assembly, where 'on vient sans façon, lire les journaux et, sous prétexte de travailler autour d'une table, causer, rire, faire ou écouter des cancans, pendant que les hommes s'escriment au whist et à l'écarté; et arrosées de quelques verres de sirop, faire des projets d'excursions pour le lendemain.'

THE CASCADE DU VALENTIN

little tired of the routine ; and this brings us to a delicate point to touch upon, the fact so tenderly dealt with by Frenchmen, that they, too, suffer from ennui. At Eaux-Bonnes, and especially at Luchon, which we shall visit by-and-by, we shall find them surrounded with almost every luxury that money can purchase, every 'distraction' that ingenuity could devise ; but the result is a failure, because the majority of French people do not care

for mountains for their own sake, or take much interest in scenery.

How little the French people really know of the Pyrenees, beyond the walks round their favourite watering-places, can only be judged of by those who have met them on their travels, and conversed much with them on such subjects.

It has been said that the modern Parisian is 'too much at ease, too much protected, that his life is scattered about in too many little delicate sensations,' that he is unfitted either physically or mentally for a mountain life, and that the true zest for the enjoyment of nature is wanting in him. Whether this be quite true or not, there is no doubt that he suffers dreadfully from ennui. M. Taine admits the fact, and says :—

'Cet ennui prouve que la vie ressemble à l'Opéra ; pour y être heureux il faut l'argent d'entrée, mais aussi *le sentiment de la musique.* Si l'argent vous manque, vous restez dehors à la pluie parmi les décrotteurs ; si le sentiment vous manque, vous dormez maussadement dans votre superbe loge.'

It is generally supposed, he goes on to say, that 'la vie aux Eaux' is very romantic, that one meets with adventures of all kinds, and above all '*aventures de cœur*' (whatever the latter may be), but he does not find it so, and is of opinion that if life here is a romance, it is only in books, and that in the Pyrenees 'great men' are more likely to be found, ' bound in calf in travellers' portmanteaus.'

In spite of the theory that in society here, conversation is 'extrêmement spirituelle,' that one meets only 'artistes, hommes supérieurs et les gens du grand monde,' that grace, elegance, and ' la fleur de tous les plaisirs,' flourish and abound, he finds the fact very different, and sums up the habits of visitors with the remark that they seem 'to wear a great many hats, to eat a great many peaches, and to talk " immensely," but that in the matter of men and ideas they differ little from the rest of the world.'

Another writer makes the following complaint about Eaux-Bonnes—' Depuis que les chemins de fer, en rapprochant les distances et en mettant les voyages à la portée d'un plus grand nombre de bourses, ont augmenté la clientèle des eaux minérales, un fait singulier s'est produit, qu'il faut citer aussi : c'est la décadence du plaisir et de la vie joyeuse à Bonnes : la foule y a remplacé l'ancienne société aristocratique.'

After this confession, the English colony at Pau can hardly be accused of being too exclusive or select.

We have been to-day, by the beautiful *Promenade de l'Impératrice*, to see the 'Cascade du Valentin,' and have met plenty of people on the way thither. There is quite an assemblage at each of the favourite places of resort, and the roar of the waterfall cannot altogether drown the voices, or the orders for 'cognac' and 'sirops' at the little café which commands the best view. The draught of air rushes down with a chilling sensation, after walking in the sun, that renders it dangerous to sit long together in one spot; yet, in spite of the cold and spray which falls like rain, we see several figures muffled in cloaks, sketching the various points of interest.

These cascades, which Murray speaks of as 'the pretty but trifling waterfalls of the Valentin,'[1] have seldom, we believe, been depicted with more power of the pencil than in the drawings by M. Doré. He has succeeded in giving the variety of form, and the undulated surface, of this enormous mass of water, as it forces its way through rocks and trees—now a broad and overwhelming cataract; now a pool of smooth water reflecting the branches of overhanging beech-trees; now escaping again in a hundred different ways, bounding from rock to rock, catching the sunshine in its course, and shedding prismatic colours on the rocks; now gathering its forces again, and roaring down into the valley far below, where

---

[1] Mr. Packe, in his most useful 'Guide to the Pyrenees,' ignores them altogether, and in other respects, scarcely, as it seems to us, does full justice to the picturesque beauty of Eaux-Bonnes.

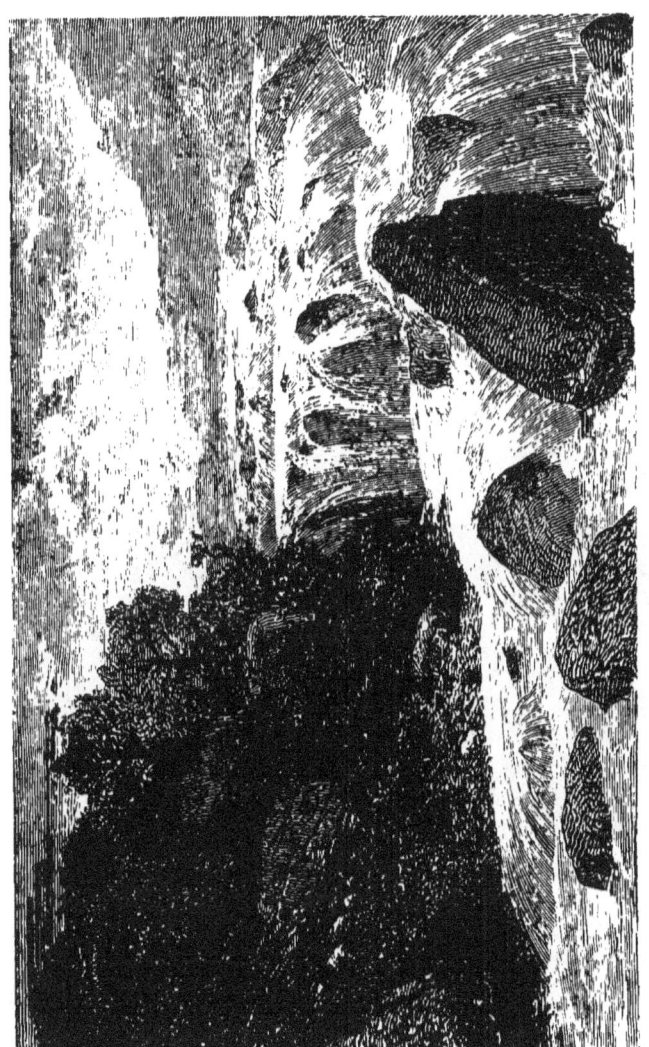

CASCADE DU VALENTIN

we can trace it in the distance, a broad river, hurrying to the sea.

We are fortunate in seeing these cascades after rain, when they are, as the French visitors express it, 'en toilette;' for, after a continuance of dry weather, they become greatly diminished, and sometimes disappear altogether.

There are walks in the neighbourhood of Eaux-Bonnes

which extend for miles, one especially above the village, to the 'plateau de la montagne verte,' from which we obtain delightful views of the mountains and valleys. The paths are for the most part shaded by trees, and it is seldom that there is not a pleasant breeze stirring, even on the hottest day.

Those of us who are accustomed to live in 'les prairies du nord,' will find even the fresh air of Eaux-Bonnes too hot for them on an August day, when there is no wind, and will do well to escape early in the morning to the heights above the town, where if fond of botany, they will find some beautiful specimens of wild flowers that are only to be met with in this and the neighbouring valleys.

The finest excursion is without doubt to the Pic de Ger, which some of our party undertook on the first fine

day after our arrival. The following notes of an ascent may be interesting :—

'August 18.—Up at 5 A.M., and having with some little difficulty selected the most soberly dressed and honest-looking guide from the crowds that danced, capered, smoked, and cracked their whips around us, we left at 5.30 A.M. for the Pic de Ger.

'After winding over several meadows we crossed the Coume d'Aas, and descended through a forest of fir to a gap in the mountain, which the guide called the Col de Valeur. Hence, turning suddenly to the left, we began to scale the steep sides of the mountain to what looked like the top. Arrived there, we found another steep and rocky ascent before us, with a stony *arête* to cross. We toiled for another half-hour, until the top was reached at 11 A.M. The view was magnificent. The Pic du Midi d'Ossau was just in front, with hundreds of the

G

THE PIC DE GER.

peaks stretching in every direction, and Eaux-Bonnes itself could just be seen, like a speck in a dark valley far beneath. A small lake was visible to the left; to the north lay the Jurançon and the table-land beyond Pau, and all around valleys and mountains—the snow-capped Vignemale rising above the rest. The height here is between 8000 and 9000 feet, and the view hence is said to be even finer than from the rival Pic du Midi d'Ossau.'

We have hitherto been speaking of Eaux-Bonnes in its summer aspect, when it is crowded and gay, but the best time to see it, and to enjoy it, is in the fine settled weather that we often have towards the middle of October, when all the little shops that lined the allées and promenades, are not only shut up, but have departed bodily and been trundled down to Pau; when the rows of seats that command the best views are untenanted; when, in short, 'la vie' has departed, and there is only one hotel open for the solitary traveller—then, indeed, there is not a more pleasant or peaceful spot in which to spend the autumn days.

We were once at Eaux-Bonnes towards the end of October, the weather was calm and fine, and warm enough for sketching out of doors without discomfort, and we remember sharing the hotel and the 'promenade horizontale' with one other visitor. He was a genial and accomplished Irishman, who had been staying here for some weeks, latterly quite alone, and in thorough enjoyment of the quiet of the place,—having come, as he said, to Eaux-Bonnes for 'constitutional' reasons. He had brought with him a well-filled purse, a weak chest, and the burden of his country's wrongs, and had come out here to take 'a calm review of the home political situation,' on the principle, we presume, that, 'C'est loin du monde qu'on peut juger sainement des illusions dont il nous environne.' Sitting under the trees on the 'Promenade' he expatiated to us for hours on the iniquity of England, in not providing his country with capital to enable it to keep pace with other nations, admitting at the same time that he spent most of his own wealth in other lands. So quaint and illogical was the reasoning, so curious was the mixture of earnestness and common sense with a sort of Quixotic romance, and so strange a contrast was he to all that had gone before, that he formed quite a feature in our recollection. The reader will pardon us if our remarks seem irrelevant—but as straws show the direction of the wind, so, if naturally and without forethought, we shall sometimes on our journey be found forgetting the mountains and turning our thoughts homeward, it is only a proof of that want of sustained interest in travelling in the Pyrenees, which in Switzerland never flags; we will not stay to analyse the subject now,—the reason may explain itself before we reach our journey's end.

We fear that in this chapter, we have fallen unconsciously into the category of other writers, and have not done justice to Eaux-Bonnes, for there is a charm about it both in summer and in autumn, that is undescribed and indescribable; an attraction altogether independent of any 'administration,' and for which we have to thank no French prefect. Those of our readers who have paid more than a passing visit here, will, we believe, agree in the above; those who have not (which expression comprises the majority of our countrymen) we would earnestly recommend to come. The natural beauty of its situation, the forms of the surrounding mountains, the variety of interest in its walks, its evergreen aspect under a July sun—its refreshing waterfalls, its delightful air, and its everchanging and wondrous view—leave an abiding sense of beauty in the mind, long after the sounds of bells, whistles, and penny trumpets; the shouts and screams, and the perpetual *fanfare* of Frenchmen making holiday, have died away.

## CHAPTER V.

### *LOURDES—ARGELÈS—CAUTERETS.*

WE now pass over into another valley to the east, to see Cauterets, one of the most ancient and populous of the Pyrenean Spas.

There are three routes, the most direct being over the 'Col de Tortes,' a steep path behind Eaux-Bonnes to the Col, nearly 6000 feet above the sea, thence descending to Arrens and Argelès, at which latter place the high road is gained between Pau and Cauterets. This route when we last passed over it was steep and fatiguing for any but good walkers, and there were parts where it was scarcely safe to keep the saddle; but a carriage road is now opened, called the *Route Thermal*, which, avoiding the summit altogether, is carried round the mountain side by a very circuitous route (in some places being built up against the almost perpendicular face of the rock), and afterwards descending by steep zigzags to Arrens.

The view from the Col de Tortes is worth the climb, and Arrens may be reached from Eaux-Bonnes by a good walker in from five to six hours. This path is altogether to be recommended in fine weather, but, yielding to the exigencies of having to take the most frequented routes, and also to visit the famous village of LOURDES, we go round by the lower road, *vià* Louvie.

Soon after seven o'clock, on one of the most lovely mornings in August, we find ourselves rolling swiftly along on a smooth high road, behind four galloping horses, the sweet morning air blowing freshly in our faces, and light fleecy clouds veiling us from the sun's rays; our position approaching much nearer to the realisation of Dr. Johnson's idea of Elysium, than that of a member of the Alpine Club. Thus we shall find it, all through the Pyrenees, and thus must picture it, to be faithful chroniclers. The ordinary mode of travelling is in two extremes, we either outrage society by shouldering a knapsack and walking off like an Arab, or glide easily through the valleys in comfortable carriages.[1]

Passing again through Laruns and Louvie Juzon, we take an easterly direction, by the picturesque little town of Lestelle, to Lourdes. The latter part of the route has been through a narrow gorge, which opens before we reach Lourdes, into the valley of Lavedan; and the river that we now see, and shall follow for many miles, is the Gave de Pau. We have left the Béarnais district, and are in the department of Bigorre.

The old historic town of Lourdes, with its gloomy castle on the heights, its old battlements and time-worn buildings, recalls many an episode of French history, and, independently of associations, is a most suggestive subject for an artist's pencil. It is situated on the high road between Pau and Cauterets, also on the railway between Pau, Bigorre, and Toulouse; several roads meet here, and overladen diligences rumble through the narrow streets all day, during the summer season.

Lourdes, situated at the edge of the plains near

---

[1] When four or five persons travel together with luggage four horses must be taken. The tariff is 40 francs a day, but an arrangement can sometimes be made at a lower rate for the whole tour of the Pyrenees.

barren mountains, unhealthy, dirty, and uninteresting, had little to attract travellers twenty years ago, excepting the historic associations connected with the fortress. It is now perhaps better known in France and more frequented by visitors and pilgrims than any other town in

the Pyrenees, on account of a miraculous vision said to have taken place here in 1858, and the healing properties of the waters.

The question is so perpetually asked in the Pyrenees, 'Have you been to Lourdes?' that we must pause on our journey to describe the place as it is to-day. The following is the story of the miracle as received at Lourdes in 1880.

In 1858 Bernadette Soubirous, the child of a Pyrenean peasant living near Lourdes, was fifteen years old ; small and childish for her age, in delicate health and uneducated. She had kept sheep on the mountains, she knew how to say her prayers ; but had had very little instruction.

One winter afternoon she went with her sister and a little girl, to gather wood. They wandered beyond the town beside the river, the younger children wading across to an island, whilst Bernadette, who wore knitted stockings as well as sabots because of her asthma, sat down on a rock, to pull them off. In the act of doing so she looked up, and above a rocky recess in the hill-side she saw the figure of a beautiful lady. This lady, as the child described her, was clothed in a white robe falling in even folds, a white veil hung down from her head on each side, round her waist a light blue sash was crossed in front, on each foot a yellow rose was blossoming. She gazed upwards, and in her hands she held a chaplet.[1]

The child fell on her knees and prayed; her companions observing her from the island saw no vision of the lady, but only Bernadette in her white woollen capulet saying her prayers, a sight in no way remarkable.

The lady disappeared, and the child described what she had seen, but of course was not believed. Again at the same time and place she saw the vision, when the lady bade her return every day for a month, told her to pray for sinners, and imparted to her several secrets which she was never to reveal. The story was quickly known in the neighbourhood, and a crowd collected. The civil authorities interfered. Bernadette was shut up, but only for a few hours, her father having promised that she should go no more to the grotto; but the ardent love and swift feet of the child carried her across the valley at the appointed time to the river-side. For some days she was ignorant as to the personality of the vision; the crowds of people watching Bernadette kneeling in ecstasy saw only the child and heard nothing. They persuaded her to ask the name of the lady, and the vision returned this remarkable answer: 'Je suis l'immaculée conception.' The child, not understanding the words, repeated them over and over to herself as she went to the curé's house in order to tell him. The priests seem to have been the last to believe in the vision. The Virgin sent a message to the curé of Lourdes by Bernadette, telling him to build her a chapel on the spot where she appeared; upon which he said if the wintry bough of wild eglantine which hung over the rock should blossom with roses, he would believe in her appearance. This was duly repeated by Bernadette, but the vision only smiled, and the frozen bough remained as before. The Virgin appeared eighteen times, and then her visits ceased entirely.

On one occasion when the vision had retreated, as she generally did into the further corner of the recess, she commanded Bernadette to eat some grass which grew there, and to scratch a hole in the soil. The child obeyed; a trickle of water issued from the ground, and gradually made its way to the entrance of the cave. The

---

[1] The images of Notre Dame de Lourdes are all represented according to this description.

wonder and interest of the crowd now greatly increased, for the water was said to have healing properties.

After the visions had ceased, marvellous cures are said to have been effected, children held in the water recovered, diseases of the eyes and injured limbs were cured. Bernadette was looked on as a saint, but does not seem to have cared for notice or distinction. During the vision it is said that she felt no bodily pain. Once holding a candle as she knelt, her hand remained in the flame without her being aware of it. However, her health soon failed, and she went far away from Lourdes, entered the Ursuline Convent at Nevers, and died there a few years ago.

On arriving at Lourdes railway station, rows of vehicles are waiting to take you to the *Grotte;* there is a separate exit for pilgrims, some of whom are arriving every day, when there is no special pilgrimage. Broad roads lead to the river where you are beset by every kind of disgusting beggar, exhibiting wounds and deformities; a bad advertisement one would think for the healing springs. The church and *Grotte* are about a mile from the railway station; on the road there is a continual traffic of vehicles, priests and peasants, women with white caps and enormous rosaries round their waists, and tourists of all countries in modern attire.

The new Gothic church, with its tall spire of white marble (built in 1868), stands prominently on the rocks above the *Grotte* and the river, some distance from Lourdes. The road from the town to the church is lined with booths for the sale of figures and statuettes of *Notre Dame de Lourdes,* in white dress and blue sash. Figures—some larger than life—half wrapped in brown paper, are exposed for sale at the booths, also enormous rosaries in black and white wood. Here the relations of the celebrated child contrive to make money out of the connection by advertising in large letters above their shops, '*tante de Bernadette,*' &c.

The church itself is approached by a flight of steps. All within is quiet; the fittings and sculpture good, and, strange to say, very little rubbish, and no tawdry altars. The walls are hung with numerous embroidered banners from the principal towns in France, from Italy, Ireland, Canada, &c.; also banners contributed by private families. The side chapels are full of votive offerings, epaulets, swords, bridal wreaths, photographs of persons cured, a bas-relief of two trains full of pilgrims meeting, the shock being averted by the appearance of the Virgin. The crypt below is full of similar offerings.

Down a pathway cut in the cliff we arrive at the river side, no longer a rough, rocky shore, but embanked with a parapet and smooth wide road; here are sheds for baths, a shop for the sale of candles, an iron railing with gates, and behind the railing the famous *Grotte*, a hole in the rock, low and shallow. In front of the rails are a few rush-bottom chairs where pilgrims kneel, also a row of ugly leaden spouts with taps, whence the water is drawn by the pilgrims in highly ornamented little flasks, and also in claret bottles.

Let us now go into the Grotte, over the low arch of which hang numbers of cast-off crutches in various stages of shabbiness. The low roof drips upon the damp floor, and a large frame of candles below drips also on the ground; the place is ghastly in the daylight, dirty with relics of departed pilgrims, and smells of grease, damp and blown-out candles.

Near at hand is a crevice full of letters directed to the Virgin, some of which appear to have been there a long time, and there are dead bouquets lying about. A woman kneeling kisses the dirty floor, and slowly sips water from a glass; two or three people sit on chairs, they look ill, and seem to be waiting patiently for their cure. They with ourselves fill the small cave, but by stooping about at the end we discover an old Bath chair with a dog coiled up inside; a wooden bed, various remnants of cast-off clothing and surgical appliances, and the *spring* itself, which is a muddy looking little pool covered with a bit of wire netting.

Perhaps it is a solemn sight to see the people creeping about, and filling their bottles, and regarding with awe the plaster cast of the 'lady' with blue sash and faded wreaths at her feet; but the 'sacred cave' with its relics fills us with disgust rather than reverence, and we are glad to get away.

People living in the neighbourhood seem to take little interest in Lourdes. They believe in the vision, and to some extent, perhaps, in the healing spring, but it is not an article of faith with them to go to Lourdes, and they prefer sending their sick to Barèges or Luchon. Strangers and pilgrims from a distance have made Lourdes what it is. In six months of the year 1859, nearly 100,000 people visited the *Grotte*, and large numbers come annually to this day.[1] *The episcopal authority is pledged to the reality of the vision*, as well as the church in distant parts of France, and the pilgrimages have the approval of the Pope.

'C'est une chance pour Lourdes,' as the landlady at quiet, beautiful Argelès remarked—a village a few miles higher up the Vallée de Lavedan, to which we now gladly turn. The branch railway from Lourdes will take us as far as Pierrefitte, but it is better to keep to the road.

On approaching Argelès, we enter a scene of pastoral

---

[1] In September, 1880, a pilgrimage was to have been conducted from England by Cardinal Manning, Duke of Norfolk and others, but was postponed, at the last moment, for political reasons.

beauty and fertility, far exceeding that of the Val d'Ossau, reminding us, in its cornfields, orchards, and woods, of a peaceful English landscape. The valley broad and well-cultivated, the Gave wide and smooth, the oak and beech trees growing luxuriantly, the wild-

flowers on banks of soft turf, the waving Indian corn, and the fresh green of the meadows—make it indeed a refreshing change from Lourdes.

Argelès, a small town where travellers used to stay but a few hours, has already become celebrated for the quiet beauty of its site, and for the comfort of the Hôtel de France. We have heard of people who have alighted here, intending to stay half-an-hour, sending for their luggage and remaining for the summer! There is so much to see in the neighbourhood of Argelès that one cannot wonder at the choice; it is certainly one of the pleasantest spots in the Pyrenees to choose for a place of residence; an oasis where English people delight to dwell. In the summer of 1880, a lady staying at Argelès thus writes: 'The Peyrafitte family, who have kept the Hôtel de France for many years, treat us as guests or personal friends. Joseph the eldest son speaks English, and is very helpful to travellers. Madame Peyrafitte walks about her pleasant dining-room (whence you can see the sunset behind the snow peaks and hear the swiftly running Gave), and watches to find out if her guests have what they really like. The guests are waited on by a band of maidens with pretty silk handkerchiefs round their heads; there are no noisy waiters at Argelès. The "Pavilion" on the opposite side of the street belongs to the hotel; it has a terrace and tier of balconies looking towards the mountains, and up the valleys to Luz and Cauterets. Coffee is served on the terrace, and we sit about on benches in the street after dinner in a delightfully easy way. There is an empty château with a wild garden next to the hotel. The villagers are pleasant and sociable, and we soon begin to know them, also the huge white Pyrenean dogs. In the salon is a collection of books, mostly English, with some French works on places in the neighbourhood, forming a pleasant library for wet days.'

The inhabitants of this part of the valley are comparatively simple and industrious, and there are fewer beggars than in the Val d'Ossau.

But to continue our journey:—

At Pierrefitte (four miles higher up the valley) we join some companions, who have come over by the mountain route from Eaux-Bonnes; and, taking fresh horses, continue our journey to Cauterets, turning up a zigzag road to the right hand, and leaving the route to Luz and Gavarnie on our left. It is a steep ascent for the first

PART OF THE VAL DE LUZ.

hour, and at several points of the road we obtain fine views of the valley through which we have just passed. Ascending slowly, we overtake a man walking by himself, who, until we come up to him, seems unaware of our approach. He is a good-looking fellow, dressed in Spanish costume, with knee breeches, a bright red sash, a dark jacket with silver buttons, and a long whip twisted and tied round his waist. We soon learn that he has taken the trouble to come all the way from Cauterets to inform us which is the best inn, where are the best horses to ride to the Lac de Gaube, when we may take the baths, &c., and, above all, *who* is the very best guide in Cauterets. He is amusing, affable, and not to be shaken off until we get into a trot again; it is useless to tell him that we have engaged our rooms, that we intend to walk to the Lac de Gaube, and to dispense with guides.

"Ces Anglais will ruin the Pyrenees!" he mutters to himself. Yes—we have added another stone to the mound of our unpopularity, by persisting, when we are on the mountains, in using our legs for walking, and our wits for finding the way.

It is nearly dusk for the rest of the journey, but we soon discern in the distance some welcome lights, and in about twelve hours after leaving Eaux-Bonnes drive into the garden in front of the Hôtel de France. The rooms are brilliantly lighted up, and in the salon we see people dancing; in the gardens and under the trees we hear laughter and the voices of women, and, here and there, little glow-worm lights betray the presence of the smoking sex.[1]

Our friend the guide, who has been riding behind,

---

[1] This by courtesy and in ignorance of facts; for we afterwards found that cigarettes were in request, both with Spanish and French ladies.

CAUTERETS

unperceived, upon our portmanteaus, now makes his appearance, and is the first to help us to alight and to show us our apartments.

Mr. Taine speaks thus of his reception and first impression of Cauterets :—

'Cauterets est un bourg au fond d'une vallée, assez triste, pavé, muni d'un octroi. Hôteliers, guides, tout un peuple affamé nous investit ; nous sommes raccrochés par des servantes, des enfants, des loueurs d'ânes, des garçons qui par hasard viennent se promener autour de nous. On nous offre des cartes, on nous vante l'emplacement, la cuisine ; on nous accompagne, casquette en main, jusqu'au bout du village ; en même temps on écarte à coups de coude des compétiteurs. " C'est mon voyageur, je te rosse si tu approches." Chaque hôtel a ses recruteurs à l'affût. Ils chassent—l'hiver à l'izard, l'été au voyageur !'

It is well to have a Frenchman's experience of Cauterets in the season ; for if we were to recount our reception the next day (which was precisely similar), when we went out into the town, it might sound like exaggeration.

Cauterets has been considerably enlarged and improved, since the above was written, but the manners and customs remain. There are upwards of two hundred houses, many lofty and well built, accommodating in the season at least two thousand visitors. The streets are crowded with people going to and from the baths ; the market is gay with the stalls of bright wools for sale, and with groups of people in Spanish costume ; rich and poor in every fantastic variety of dress, including priests with broad-brimmed hats, and brown Capuchin friars ; and, as a background, any number of muleteers, guides, pedlars, and idlers, lolling about or sitting in the sun.

Saddle horses and carriages for hire stand about in abundance, and there is generally a crowd round a party of Frenchmen who are preparing to start on some expedition. These starts are arranged in the middle of the high road, and sometimes take half an hour.

There is nothing more charming than the rides in this neighbourhood. The air is fresh, and feels unusually bracing for the Pyrenees; there is almost always a breeze coming down the valley, and you may ride under the shade of trees and through woods for hours.

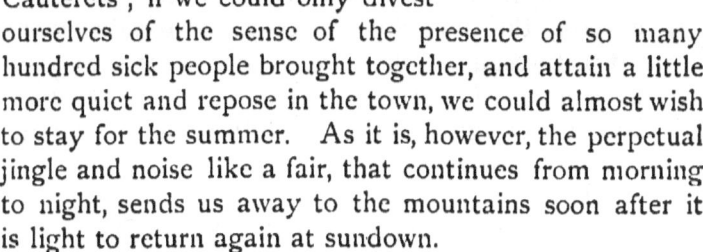

No wonder that our ancestors, who came here for the healing waters, speak in such praise of Cauterets; if we could only divest ourselves of the sense of the presence of so many hundred sick people brought together, and attain a little more quiet and repose in the town, we could almost wish to stay for the summer. As it is, however, the perpetual jingle and noise like a fair, that continues from morning to night, sends us away to the mountains soon after it is light to return again at sundown.

With the bathing, we who come to see the country have really little to do, and in spite of the celebrity of the springs of Cauterets, must give them only a passing allusion.

There are several sources of the waters, varying in temperature and slightly in composition. The Établissement called *La Raillère*, which is considered one of the most efficacious in pulmonary complaints, is built upon a raised terrace about a mile from the town, at the foot of Mont Regnère, a granite mountain almost destitute of trees, to and from which carriages, omnibuses and sedan chairs are passing with patients all day. The thermal building at La Raillère comprises 'twenty-three cabinets de bain, a fountain for the water-drinkers, an ascending and descending douche, a large peristyle with marble arches, and an extensive terrace in which to take exercise in dry or wet weather.'

The extraordinary cures effected by the hot sulphureous springs of Cauterets are the constant theme of conversation in the Pyrenees, and they are particularly esteemed by Spaniards, who come here in great numbers.

The best excursion in the neighbourhood—the chief reason for coming to Cauterets—is to see one of the few lakes of which the Pyrenees can boast, the Lac de Gaube (5866 feet above the sea), for there is nothing we miss so much, in the scenery of the Pyrenees, as the lakes reflecting the blue sky. Even the waterfalls, numerous and picturesque as they are, appear somewhat insignificant compared with those of Switzerland, although there is a softness and luxuriant beauty in their surroundings that compensates in great measure for any lack of grandeur.

It takes about two hours and a half to reach the Lac de Gaube, the path is easily found, and is well trodden during the season. Leaving the valley of Latour (in which Cauterets is situated) on our left hand, the road, passing La Raillère in about a quarter of an hour, ascends, first gradually through a wood and by several cascades, then through pine-forests by a steep path for about six miles, to the Pont d'Espagne. Here we make a halt before crossing into Spain, and wander about

amongst the moss-grown rocks and débris through which the Gave rushes down, casting up a shower of spray which keeps the trees and shrubs in perpetual freshness.

From the Pont d'Espagne to the Lac de Gaube, is about two miles,—first by a steep ascent leading through a pine wood, thence over a path strewn with rocks and loose stones,—and in a little less than an hour we reach the mountain lake, so solitary, so still, and so different from anything yet seen as to take us by surprise. It is about two miles and a half in circumference, and is said to be the largest lake in the Pyrenees. At one end is a little cabin, and hard by, on a rock, a white marble monument to the memory of an Englishman and his wife who were drowned here when on their wedding tour. The guides and the people who live in the little cabin tell the story, and, almost in the same breath, ask if we will not take a row across the lake.

On our way hither we have passed several parties on foot and on horseback, but now that we have arrived at the lake we see no one; they have all retired to a hut near at hand to breakfast on the lake trout, and leave us to the quiet enjoyment of the place.

The Lac de Gaube is a perfect mountain-basin, the water being prevented from escaping into the valley by a natural granite wall, which forms an embankment at the northern end. From this point we obtain a grand view of the snow-covered Vignemale, reflected in the still water. The sides of the lake are steep and rugged, with black masses of fir trees reaching almost to the water's edge, making a dark sombre foreground. At the upper end of the lake, we can just trace the waterfall which winds down from its glacier source; and if we were to sleep in the little cabin, and row across the lake

PONT D'ESPAGNE

in early morning, we might, with a good guide, reach the summit of one at least of the snowy peaks we see in the illustration (between 10,000 and 11,000 feet), commanding a more extensive view than from the Maledetta, or other accessible mountain of the high Pyrenees.

The variety and beauty of the excursions in the neighbourhood of the Lac de Gaube, and the pleasant valley of Cauterets, by woods and waterfalls, to the snow-clad summits of the great chain, have detained many of our countrymen for weeks, and it is only to be regretted that we have still but imperfect information about some of the routes. The local guides prefer keeping to the beaten tracks, and require much persuasion and good pay, before undertaking any new expedition.

There is one excursion that should not be missed by those who are good climbers, and are favoured with clear weather, viz., to the Lac d'Estom, Soubiran, by the Valley of Latour. Dr. Taylor thus speaks of it:—

'Here, in the month of July, accompanied by two friends, we found ourselves in the neighbourhood of the snow regions. Nothing could be more bleak or desolate than this spot. No vestige of a human habitation, or of human beings, with the exception of two goatherds who had in the summer months spent their youth and manhood in this desert, and did not recollect one party, during fourteen years, who had proceeded to the upper lake. However, being determined to make the attempt, we induced one of the goatherds to guide us, and commenced the ascent of one of the most uninviting mountains in creation (a near neighbour of the Vignemale, and little inferior in height), where our first essay at ascending was over a bridge of snow, with a torrent running beneath.

LAC DE GAUBE.

'After two or three hours of toilsome labour, we gained one of the crests of the mountains, and had the satisfaction to see on the other side, many hundred feet beneath us, the Lac d'Estom, Soubiran, completely frozen over, and this in the south of France, a few miles from Spain, and on the 6th of July!'

We quote the above as a suggestion to others staying at Cauterets for any length of time, because those who have made the ascent long after Dr. Taylor, all concur in the extraordinary interest attaching to this excursion, for which the short allusion in guide-books hardly prepares travellers. It is well to add, that it is positively dangerous in bad or uncertain weather.

Every day during our stay is occupied in some picturesque excursion in the environs, and every evening we are launched on a sea of small dissipations, the like of which we could not have imagined possible on the steep side of a mountain 3000 feet above the level of the sea. It is one continual round of dancing, singing, promenading and, we may add, flirting—everything to make us forget the mountains, and much to remind us of Paris. Only one evening differed from the rest, which we will describe as we put it down at the time.

Just a little weary of 'life' at Cauterets — life as represented by the interminable bathing and promenading, and by the little songs and dances of which the evenings are made up—we venture into the 'salon de lecture,' to see what is there provided for amusement or instruction.

In most of the principal hotels in the Pyrenees there is a large apartment, sometimes forty or fifty feet long, handsomely furnished with clocks and moderator lamps, with rich hangings to the windows, and a profusion of uncomfortable chairs. The floor is waxed and slippery;

in the centre there is a little table, like an island, with the papers of the day upon it, and in one corner, some book-shelves containing the 'library'; everything provided sumptuously for guests that never come. There is solitude in this room any evening in the height of the season; through the open windows we hear, indeed, the distant whistles and drums of civilisation, but we share the vast salon with a bat.

The pile of newspapers consists almost entirely of literature intended for visitors to 'Les Eaux,' and is earnestly devoted to advertising the various watering-places of France. Their titles are suggestive enough, viz.:—

| | |
|---|---|
| 'Gazette des Eaux.' | 'Echos de l'Adour.' |
| 'Nymphe des Eaux.' | 'Revue de Luchon.' |
| 'Moniteur des Eaux.' | 'Indicateur de Pau.' |
| 'Le Monde Thermal.' | 'Nouvelles de Cauterets.' |
| 'Mémorial des Pyrénées.'[1] | 'Journal des Chasseurs;' |

nearly all belonging to the butterfly order, having a short life and a merry one, spreading their wings in summer time and then disappearing altogether. Illustrations, and caricatures by Cham, are great features, and the headings to the papers themselves are curiosities —one having a picture of the rising sun upon it, and the motto '*Il paraît tous les jours!*' The 'feuilletons' are rich in literature of a sensational description. The readers of one journal are promised that the exciting tale of 'Le Vagabond,' is to be followed by another entitled, 'Crime et Châtiment—a tale of horror,' &c. There are scraps of politics, not very new, nor always very intelligible; thus, under the heading of 'Chronique,'

---

[1] The 'Mémorial des Pyrénées' is the best local paper.

we read that 'Europe is agitated and trembles;' there is a vague feeling that great events 'se preparent'! &c. Under the heading of 'Étranger,' we have the following news from Chili :—

'Les RR. PP. Jésuites, having persuaded the young women of Santiago to place themselves in direct epistolary correspondence with the Virgin, a special box has been attached to the doors of the churches for the reception of letters.'

There are two illustrations to this last piece of intelligence, one representing a lady hesitatingly consigning a letter to the 'Buzon de la Vírgen,' a box decorated with lace and flowers; another, called 'Departure of letters for the Holy Virgin,' where two priests are seen burning letters on a salver held high in the air!

Besides the 'news,' there are selections of original poetry, conundrums, and puffs of tradesmen in abundance; but the most interesting piece of intelligence is to be found under the heading of '*Nouvelles de Cauterets*,' being an account of a young lady of 'high position and princely liberality,' who—imitating the days of the Trianon, when Marie Antoinette and the ladies of her court went about disguised as milkmaids—attended the fêtes here in the dress of a peasant girl, but who, truth to tell, had so many admirers in her 'simple but piquante' attire, that she was forced to beat a rapid retreat. A column and a half of the '*Journal de Cauterets*' is devoted to a description of this young and beautiful Hungarian countess, who, in her simple peasant's dress, and handkerchief tied coquettishly round her head (armed with a few sentences in the patois of the valley 'to keep off the shepherds!') joined the fête champêtre, and acted her character with 'the most perfect simplicity!'

'What is the use of being young, charming, rich and

titled if one may not have a few caprices?' asks the journalist, with delightful naïveté; ending his praises by holding up the young lady as a pattern to all 'baigneuses' present, and to come, on account of her generosity. Perhaps it is cynical to suggest it, but the whole reads very like a puff, when it concludes with a list of her good deeds; how she gave 100 francs to the church, 100 francs towards the fête, &c., and how, on the day of her departure, she left a handsome sum for the benefit of the poor of Cauterets.

The library in the salon contained a few books of reference, but the bulk of the mental pabulum was made up as follows, reading hastily through the titles:—

'Un Chevalier d'Amour.'
'Les Femmes d'Aujour-d'hui.'
'Les Gandins (Mystère du Demi-Monde).'
'La Voleuse d'Amour.'
'Le Dernier Amour.'
'Une Parvenue.'
'Les Amours du Vert-Galant.'
'Les Belles Pêcheresses.'
'Les Cours Galantes.'
'Entre Deux Femmes.'
'Les Errants de Nuit.'

All through the week—every evening during our stay at Cauterets—a sort of fair was kept up; and we could not have believed, if we had not seen it for ourselves, that such a collection of trinkets, toys, and trumpery from the Palais Royal, could have been here brought together.

We had donkey races, running in sacks, and climbing poles; there were 'courses de cruches,' races with vessels full of water carried on the heads of young girls, most of whom were drenched in a most pitiless manner; whilst one, 'Mademoiselle Sophie,' the most active and spirited of the party, carried off a prize of 10 francs for having maintained the 'cruche en équilibre.'

Our remembrances of Cauterets are (independently of the fair) of an expensive residence, of a most fashionable promenade, of the noises of whips cracking, pianos jingling, of singing, of smoking ad libitum; of tall men riding diminutive ponies, and 'les grandes dames,' gaily caparisoned mules; of the town looking as if it was perpetually going out to dinner in sedan chairs, of salons, of 'journals pour rire et pour instruire,' with articles diluted to holiday calibre, of cascades and springs, of water—water, everywhere; of English scrambling up the

rocks, of Frenchmen 'en promenade,' and of Spaniards sitting under the trees.

Our thoughts, if we analyse them, are not so much of the mountains and of the pine-forests that overhang its streets, as of smooth lawns and parterres; not of torrents, but of the prettiest artificial cascades; not of rocks in their natural beauty, but of granite, smoothed and 'faced,' and turned into dwellings for the lords of the creation; of waters bottled off and stamped with the seal of the republic; and of the very stones at the road-side, numbered and registered like citizens of France.

In short, everything was civilised at Cauterets, they had civilised a bear; and nothing will leave a more mournful memory, not even the tragedy at the Lac de Gaube, than the picture of this dancing bear (performing almost in sight of his comrades in the mountains), and of his fellow in misfortune, the monkey that took the money.

A satire upon society—a thing to be remembered, was the appearance of this last little figure, a type of the artificial atmosphere of the place—the 'fun of the fair' for one sou; a strange, sad-looking being (wearing a red 'beret' on his head and a bright embroidered sash), with very little of the animal about him—altogether a forlorn and most dissipated-looking little monkey, thus over-dressed and out of his element—the image, in little, of many who crowd round him, the perfect type of 'la vie!'

## CHAPTER VI.

### *STORM.*

'La gorge était illuminée dans ses profondeurs ; ses blocs entassés, ses arbres accrochés aux roches, ses ravines déchirées, son Gave écumant, apparaissaient dans une blancheur livide, et s'évanouissaient comme les visions fugitives d'un monde tourmenté et inconnu. 'Bientôt la grande voix du tonnerre roula dans les gorges ; les nuages qui le portaient rampaient à mi-côté et venaient se choquer entre les roches ; la foudre éclatait comme une décharge d'artillerie ; le vent se leva et la pluie vint.'—*Taine.*

IT is not uncommon for travellers who have come to the mountains in summer time for health and recreation, and whose only chance of enjoyment is the continuance of fine weather, to regard with something of anxiety the clouds gathering round the distant peaks ; and it is also not uncommon for them to see, at the same time, a long procession headed by a priest, winding slowly up the valley.

The country, green and bright as it looks, is really suffering from drought, and, as a last resource, the curé, or priest, has been appealed to ; the hat is handed round, money is subscribed liberally, a mass is celebrated, and—in due time, the rain comes.

In our wanderings in the Val d'Ossau and the Val de Luz, we had frequently noticed traces of the ravages of storms, and in the windings of the Gave, the marks where in many places it had overflowed its banks; but the beauty of the weather, which continued day by day with almost a monotony of sunshine and blue sky, and the calm and peaceful aspect of security with which the inhabitants seemed to be gathering their harvest and tending their flocks, left us quite unprepared for the startling change that a few hours brought about.

The following, from our note-book, may give a more vivid impression of the scene than anything we could re-write.

The morning had been fine and cloudless, as usual, with a sun almost as powerful as in the tropics; it was too hot to do anything, apparently, but work in the fields as the women and young girls were doing, some bare-headed and barefooted, binding the sheaves of Indian corn, and struggling under loads of hay, that an English labourer would hesitate to carry.

There was little to indicate a coming storm within half an hour of its breaking, but then the signs were unmistakable and not to be disregarded.

First of all, a few little clouds were seen to gather at the head of the valley in a wild uncertain manner, and every now and then we heard trees rustling in the wind higher up the mountains, although not a leaf stirred near us; presently we seemed encompassed by four winds at once, and the dust and leaves, and sheaves of corn, were whirled up in the air with the suddenness of an explosion. The sun was still shining brightly, and there were few clouds overhead, but, as if with a sudden instinct of self-preservation, every living thing in the valley and on the mountains hurried home. The women left the fields, the men their work in the forests, the birds were silent, the dogs disappeared, the cattle of their own accord drew away to shelter, higher up the valley, and

I

even the pigs (who sleep in companies by the roadside) roused themselves for once and shuffled home.

In the narrow street of a little village some goats are hustling and struggling, under the heels of a sullen grey pony, who, with his forefeet planted firmly on the ground, and his mane and tail spread out by the wind, stands immovable, without a purpose apparently but obstruction. A few of the most active of the inhabitants are tying their carts and implements to the trunks of trees, and stowing away loose timber, but the majority are engaged in barring their doors, or peering furtively from dark windows and apertures, in a manner that suggests a Poussin or a Teniers.

But now all interest is centred in the approaching storm, and it is a difficult task to describe the change, the almost dramatic suddenness, with which a sunny smiling valley is turned into a howling wilderness. A

shadow should be cast over these pages, something more expressive than words, more powerful than Doré's pencil, should be enlisted in the service, and something should be done, were it possible, to give the moaning of the wind. The sound is piteous, and now almost constant, interrupted only by thunder, and the distant roar of waterfalls.

The sun has not quite left the lower part of the valley, but the mountain-tops are in darkness, excepting when a sudden lightning flash reveals their outlines for a moment.

Another ten minutes and the clouds come down, closing over us, like a dark veil stretched completely across the valley. The wind that fanned us so gently but an hour since, sweeps past with the noise and fury of battle, bending the tall pine-trees as it passes over them, dashing the waterfalls into spray, and scattering far and wide the sheaves of corn. Suddenly another element is added—a downpour as of a cataract, swelling the Gave to a roaring torrent, which now joins in the tumult.

Let us see what havoc is being made on its banks. Following its windings as far as we can discern through the clouds and rain, there are several companies of weather-beaten pines, against which the storm is raging in all its fury. As the clouds pass over they are continually concealed from view, as if in the smoke of battle, every here and there their ranks appearing—now resisting, now falling, bending, or snapping before the blast, but generally reappearing with a persistence that suggests to the spectator something human and heroic in the fight. Nothing, however, that we have yet seen—not the grandeur of the storm, its suddenness, or its power of destruction—is so extraordinary as the mass of water which has risen on every side. The lower parts of the valley have become one vast lake, dotted with island tree-tops, haystacks, timber, and wrecks of all kinds, carried down by the flood. The villages built on rising

THE BATTLE OF THE TREES.

ground (with foreknowledge of these disasters), escape the deluge, but many outlying buildings and parts of the road have altogether disappeared. In scarcely less time than it takes to write it, we see acres of water where there were cultivated fields, and the rain that came with the thunder and the wind, now falls steadily and straight like a waterspout.

In half an hour all is again changed, the rain ceases as suddenly as it came, the mist clears, and the clouds drift away through the trees. The sides of the valley are streaked with torrents looking like veins of silver, every little cascade has become for the time a torrent, and the Gave, now dark, muddy, and turbulent, burdened with floating timber and débris of all kinds, has scarcely any limit, for there is water everywhere.

As soon as the storm had ceased, the water seemed to subside in the upper part of the valley almost as rapidly as it had risen, but the scene here was, if possible, more desolate, from the havoc that had been made amongst the trees in exposed situations. One point was very striking, where there was a piece of pasture-land separated on either side by a narrow gorge. This promontory was a complete mountain-wreck; it had been exposed to the full fury of two winds meeting in their downward course, and everything had 'gone by the board'; trees were stripped of their branches, torn down, snapped and twisted into strange fantastic shapes, scarcely a whole stem out of a regiment of stately pines; nothing but waifs and strays, like a harvest-field given up to the gleaners. Nothing was to be heard at this spot but the rushing of water, no human being was in sight, no cattle had returned to pasture, nothing living apparently, save two young eagles that flew low in the valley, and a solitary lizard (who had had much more water than was good for him) that came out of his hiding-place, and spread a spangled S upon the rock. Then when the clouds had gathered up from the valley, there came a stream of light from the west, that, glancing from the rocks and torrents on either side, fell full upon this promontory,

gilding the stems of the shattered pines, and marking in characters only too distinct the devastating work of storms.

A few hours only and the waters will subside, and it will again be 'summer in the Pyrenees.'

A word about Doré's illustrations of these storms, which seem to us, some of the finest works of the kind he has ever achieved. As we stood in our secure shelter, watching, what it did not require much stretch of the

AFTER THE STORM

imagination to picture as a battle, we confess to have been completely carried away by the human aspect of the fight, *before we had seen the drawings*, and can hardly agree with those who think that in depicting such subjects, M. Doré has given too much scope to his fancy.

There is a parallel to it, which we must be pardoned for alluding to in passing, a scene of even greater interest, which is enacting any stormy autumn day, not so very far from us, here, on the North African shore, where a group of palm-trees have stood guard for more than a hundred years over Mahommedan tombs. To see these giants battling with the storm, crashing against each other, swaying and moaning in the wind, with their plumed heads bowed and dishevelled, their dead comrades lying at their feet, is something more fearful than the battle of the pines, but of precisely the same human and dramatic character.

And the sunset after the storm, which is one of the grandest sights in the Pyrenees, calls to mind even more vividly the same group of palm-trees, not in war but in peace—when their dark funereal plumes (tattered and weather-stained, like the colours and trophies of battle) are tinged with a deep orange hue, and we see

> 'The grace and glory of their feathery branches
> Spread like wings that love the light,'

and wish that any words of ours could induce some English landscape painters to depict such scenes—scenes, worthy of the full expression of a poet's heart, either by his pencil or his pen.

## CHAPTER VII.

### VAL DE LUZ—GAVARNIE—BRÈCHE DE ROLAND.

THE approach to Luz and St. Sauveur by the Gorge de Pierrefitte is of a wild and desolate character, which the ruins of castles on the heights seem rather to increase, giving it altogether a different aspect to the valley near Argelès.

In order to reach St. Sauveur from Cauterets, we have had, as usual, to retrace our steps, this time only a distance of about eight miles, as far as Pierrefitte, where we turn southwards again, entering the gorge, of which the next illustration will convey some idea.

At one point the road is carried along a ledge of rock which overhangs the Gave, and for some distance we pass between two walls of rock, which resemble the Via Mala on the passage of the Splügen, only that within a few yards of this stern region, the sides of the mountains are covered with foliage, with heath, ferns, ivy, and multitudes of small creeping plants, including the blue columbine which grows in abundance, and that in a few hours we shall arrive, not as in Switzerland, at a hospice where friendly monks come through the snow to receive us, but at the door of a 'grand hôtel,' where there is the best *dîner à la russe* to be had in the Pyrenees,

GORGE DE PIERREFITTE

and where the valley echoes to the serenades of villagers welcoming newcomers.

When the valley expands again, several miles from Pierrefitte, we see before us the old town of Luz, and keeping to the right, or the western side of the valley, we arrive at the village of St. Sauveur, consisting of a long street of lodging-houses and hotels, built on a

ST. SAUVEUR.

ledge of rock above the Gave, as we see in the illustration. There is accommodation for upwards of three hundred people, and the situation is charming; the walks and rides in the neighbourhood surpassing in variety and extent almost any other watering-place.

A BIRD'S-EYE VIEW.

Luz and St. Sauveur are within a mile of each other, the latter being at the foot of the beautiful valley leading to Gavarnie. St. Sauveur is a very popular watering-place, created, so to speak, by the late Empress of the French, and has been crowded with visitors whenever we have seen it.

We might have arrived at St. Sauveur from Cauterets by a mountain-path, a regular Alpine scramble, taking longer than the carriage-road, but we should have missed the Gorge de Pierrefitte, and obtained instead a 'bird's-eye view' as in the illustration. 'Of all these bird's-eye views over the High Pyrenees desolation is the prevailing characteristic,' says an Alpine traveller. 'When perched upon these aërial summits, in the midst of the Hautes Pyrénées, we can see nothing around us but long desolate ridges, scored and broken by torrents; vegetation lies crouching in the hollows, and the bare bones of this wonderful earth meet the eye.'

'The descent to Luz,' he adds, 'by the village of Grust, proved much longer than I had expected, but the views were grand, and the slopes not difficult, and covered with wild flowers.'

Perhaps we have altogether spent much more time on the high passes than in the valleys, but every year we become more impressed with the conviction that a mountain, like a monument, was intended to be seen from below, and that views from great heights and from mountain-tops are generally failures, when objects lose their beauty of form, and there is little or nothing to guide the eye to any distinct distance or perspective.

We must now leave the neighbourhood of St. Sauveur, and passing over the new stone bridge which spans the

Gave with one magnificent arch, walk up the valley by the right bank of the river towards GAVARNIE.

'Il est enjoint,' says Taine, 'à tout être vivant et pouvant monter un cheval, un mulet, un quadrupède quelconque, de visiter Gavarnie ; à défaut d'autres bêtes, il devrait, tout haute cessant, enfourcher un âne.' But a good carriage-road has now been completed all the way to Gavarnie, and there are numerous conveyances passing up and down in the summer.

It is said—but the same thing has been said so often of different parts of the Pyrenees, that we almost fear to repeat the remark—that this valley is alone worth coming to see. Certainly at a point a few miles up, where Doré has made his sketch (now spanned by a fine new bridge), we can imagine nothing more beautiful, or a more charming combination of woods and rocks, waterfalls and mountain forms, than this view—one quite unattainable from the heights of which we have just been speaking.

Crossing over the bridge, and now keeping to the left bank of the stream, passing on our route the ruins of an old fort, and through a narrower and wilder part of the valley, we come to an open space, or basin, called Pragnères ; then through the gorge of Trimbareille to the village of Gèdres (where the valley expands again) at the entrance of another valley leading to Héas, a little mountain village, consisting of a church—one building that may be called a house, and two or three small hovels. It is, however, a most convenient spot from which to approach the great chain near the Pic des Aiguillons, affording, according to good authority, 'homely refreshment, and two available beds.'

Leaving Gèdres, and continuing up the valley, passing

OLD BRIDGE AT SUS

on our right hand a beautiful cascade, we enter upon a scene which it is scarcely possible to describe, so utterly different is its aspect from any ordinary phase of nature.

On the other side of the Pyrenees, on the high road to Madrid, the traveller passes for miles over mountains covered with a wilderness of loose rocks and stones, lying scattered and heaped up pell-mell, without any apparent reason or design; but he is hurried through the dreary landscape by railway, and soon forgets the aspect of this forsaken-looking land. Here, on the path to Gavarnie, the pedestrian comes, gradually, upon a

CHAOS.

scene of grandeur and wild confusion, which is almost terrible to contemplate; the road, winding through a

FORES

maze of giant boulders, which seem to have been cast about as if in some fearful explosion—we say explosion, because it is difficult, otherwise, to give any idea of the confused aspect of the rocks.[1]  We see nothing like the traces of an ordinary upheaving of nature, and few marks of glaciers; everything is as its name implies, *chaos*, a group of mountain fragments thrown down like hail, turning the bed of the valley into a ruin.

In about an hour and a half after leaving Gèdres we reach Gavarnie, a little mountain village, consisting of a few huts and one comfortable inn.  It is 4380 feet above the sea, and is a most delightful place to stay at in summer, to explore the glaciers and neighbouring mountains.  The air is fresh and invigorating, having that crisp, bracing, mountain-feeling, if we may use the expression, that is seldom experienced in the Pyrenees at the same altitude.

When we arrived, there were a few guides sitting about in the sun; and in the inn, one traveller, the author of the 'Guide to the Pyrenees,' a book which has perhaps done more than any other to popularise these mountains amongst Englishmen.  During our stay he was the only other occupant of the inn, and it was a source of great regret that circumstances prevented our joining him in several expeditions, to the higher chain, which he was making alone.  Mr. Packe said that he generally made Gavarnie his head-quarters in the summer; that he had been here several months, and was now leaving for a few weeks, to return again.

There is something about the life of this solitary

---

[1] Some of these single boulders are the size of a house; many of them are grass-grown, or covered with moss and lichen, and in cavities where there is a little soil, the box-tree grows out of their sides.

Englishman amongst the mountains, that seems to us pathetically interesting, because, notwithstanding all he has done to lay down routes and add to our knowledge of the natural beauties of the Pyrenees, he has but few sympathisers and scarcely any followers, even amongst his *confrères*, the members of the Alpine Club. When we consider how he has devoted himself to exploring these mountains, in the face of numerous obstacles, not the least of these being the ignorance of the peasantry, and the want of guides who know the higher Alps (or if knowing them who will not act as guides), it is disheartening to find so few men following his example.

But we, English people, have not yet taken to these mountains, and made them a playground. Until we do this, and encourage the race of guides, now fast springing up, and tempt speculators to build hotels on such spots as Gavarnie, or 'Super Bagnères' near Luchon; until we explode the guide-book prejudice that the Pyrenees are unhealthy, and come out here every summer, with our knapsacks, to take quiet possession of 'les hautes Pyrénées,' not intruding our tweeds and wide-awakes unnecessarily at such places as Cauterets or Luchon, but keeping to our work—not until we do this, but when we do—we shall create a passion for climbing in the Pyrenees that will almost vie with Switzerland.

There is one thing wanting yet, a new edition of Mr. Packe's guide-book and a better map of the Central Pyrenees; other maps, in fact, like the one in his book, of the district to the south of Luchon. We might ask further, that the next new 'Handbook,' or 'new edition,' should tell us more about the high passes, and about the Spanish side of the Pyrenees, which so few have

CHAOS.

leisure or opportunity to explore, and from which the uncertainty of the weather has so often driven people back. At present, there is no modern work that does this completely, or that describes the Central Pyrenees in the same genial, hearty, and enthusiastic manner, that is peculiar to the literature of Switzerland.

The purpose of the present volume being confined to a description of the most popular routes—following in the footsteps of M. Doré—we have been compelled to omit the accounts of many excursions in the higher Alps.

We must now say a few words about the Cirque de Gavarnie, and the 'Brèche de Roland.' The extraordinary semicircle of rocks, called the Cirque—celebrated for its unique beauty, celebrated in the annals of many a smuggling expedition from Spain, celebrated in song, and historically associated with notable men, amongst others with the great French caricaturist Paul Chevalier, who here took his well-known *nom de plume*—rises before us a vast rampart dividing France and Spain, the upper serrated ridge of which, the redoubtable Roland is said, in a legend, to have ridden up to, and cut through with his sword, in his eagerness to pursue the Moors. How he crossed the glacier on horseback is not explained, nor is the story clear in other particulars, but it is too popular to omit all mention of.

We obtain a good view of the Cirque in half an hour after leaving the inn, but it is a walk of several miles, over a path strewn with rocks and débris before we reach the Cirque itself, or the position on the rocks, where the sketch, on the next page, was taken. There are numerous cascades down the precipitous sides of the rocks, the principal one falling about twelve hundred

THE CIRQUE DE GAVARNIE.

feet, and there is no sound but that of the waters playing upon the polished marble surface of the rocks, which in sunlight, and especially at sunset, cast the most beautiful prismatic gleams across the Cirque.

This fall is said, erroneously, to be the highest in Europe; it is certainly imposing, but in summer, when most visitors see it, the water is diminished to what scarcely appears a continuous thread. As these cascades appear to better advantage from a distance, it is scarcely worth the trouble of scrambling over the rocks to approach their base, excepting for the purpose of searching for fossils or rare botanical specimens, which are often to be found near this spot; but it is worth waiting until the evening, near the cabin shown in the next illustration, to see the sun's rays upon the spray, when the snow is lighted up with a rose-coloured hue, and the dark masses of fir-trees and the shadows cast across the Cirque, make a sombre foreground.

For the following account of the ascent of the Brèche

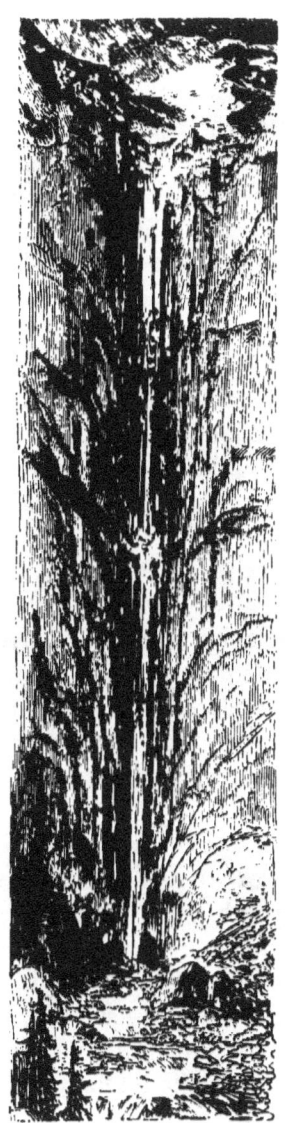

de Roland we are indebted to a member of the Alpine Club :—

'Left Gavarnie at five A.M., and stopped at the little inn near the Cirque, where we got a guide, and set off for the ascent of the Brèche de Roland. Any way up the steep face of the rock, just opposite the waterfall, seems quite impracticable; but you find hand-and-foot hold of a buttress that is formed of slabs of rock, which appear set on end ; and up the crumbling wall you toil for an hour until you gain its top, when the walking becomes easy, over smooth slabs of rock and green patches of moss. All around the ground seems to have been subjected to some immense volcanic action; the curious position and shaly burnt look of the rocks and boulders were remarkable. The view hence is very fine, the waterfall especially looks to great advantage from the heights, and the snowy masses of the Vignemale and the Mont Perdu, are a fitting background.

'We soon lost sight of the Cirque, with its streaming glaciers and dark battlements, and began the ascent of a long slope of snow, the Brèche lying to our left. This appeared going out of the way, but the steep angle at which the glacier that leads up to it is inclined made it necessary to turn it. Having arrived nearly at the top of the slope, we turned sharp to the left, cutting steps sideways in the glacier. This was slow, *hot*, tiresome work, but it is soon crossed, and in a few moments you reach the Brèche de Roland. The view is very fine—on one side France, on the other side Spain—lying as it were at your feet ; the Pic du Midi de Bigorre, conspicuous to the north-east ; to the south, mountain on mountain, and valley on valley, stretched away for miles over the Peninsula, its hazy, stony and barren appearance being most remarkable.

'Les seuls habitants sont les cascades, assemblées pour former le Gave.'

'On descending, we saw the cavern where people sleep on making the ascent of Mont Perdu, which mountain lay to our left; then, recrossing the glacier, descended the snow-slope by a glissade, and afterwards the wall of

ASCENT OF THE PIC DE BERGONS.

rock (coming down being much more fatiguing than going up), reaching Gavarnie about four P.M.'

Taking advantage of a return carriage the next day, which had brought some visitors to Gavarnie, we soon rattle down over the newly-made road, and past the wonderful chaos, to St. Sauveur and Luz; in time to join a party who are going to ascend the 'Pic de Bergons' to see the sunset. It is one of the easiest, and at the same time one of the best worth undertaking, of any mountain excursion in this part of the Pyrenees. From the summit (only 6791 feet) we see to the south, the Mont Perdu, and the Brèche de Roland above the Cirque de Gavarnie, and obtain the best general view of the range of limestone mountains that form the crest or backbone of the great chain.

We will not detain the reader with details of this ascent, which, although wild and striking in parts, especially where M. Doré has taken his sketch (p. 141), presents no real difficulties to the climber, and on this occasion admitted of few adventures beyond slips and tumbles, and a long chase after a wide-awake, which a sudden gust of wind whirled upwards and over a chasm.

It is a most popular expedition, and in fine weather we may see almost as many adventurous mountaineers as in the illustrations; but fine clear weather is rare, and we may ascend over and over again without getting any view. We may have been sitting under the trees, or taking shelter from the sun all day in the valley, but no sooner do we get to any altitude than the clouds pursue us like fate, enveloping everything in a damp shroud, through which we cannot see many yards before us, and from which we only emerge on returning to the valley.

It is considered a triumphant thing amongst the habitués of St. Sauveur or Luz to have made an 'ascension' of any kind, but to have seen either sunrise or sunset under favourable conditions from the Pic de Bergons is almost too much good fortune to hope for on one's first visit. M. Taine discourses thus pleasantly on these 'ascensions':—

'J'étais un jour sur une montagne avec une famille, à qui le guide montrait une ligne bleuâtre indistincte, en disant: "Voilà Toulouse!" Le père, les yeux brillants, répétait aux fils: "Voilà Toulouse!" Ceux-ci, voyant cette joie, criaient avec transport: "Voilà Toulouse!" Ils apprenaient à sentir le beau, comme on apprend à saluer, par tradition de famille. C'est ainsi qu'on forme des artistes, et que les grands aspects de la nature impriment pour jamais dans l'âme de solennelles émotions!'

ANCIENT CHURCH OF THE TEMPLARS AT LUZ.

## CHAPTER VIII.

### *LUZ—BARÈGES—BAGNÈRES DE BIGORRE.*

THE situation of Luz, in a large natural basin surrounded on all sides by mountains, is preferred by many visitors to St. Sauveur. It is more open, and the walks are more varied; it is less fashionable and pretentious, and once was much cheaper than St. Sauveur as a place of residence. But partly from its central situation (as may be seen on the map), partly from the fame of Madame Cazeaux's dinners at the Hôtel des Pyrénées, and chiefly from the report of its cheapness, it has now become dear; and we doubt if M. Taine saw it in its crowded, noisy state to-day, with its modern white houses and hotels, he would be disposed to call it any longer a 'petit village, tout rustique.'

An old fortified church, built in the time of the Templars, where service is still performed behind its ramparts, and the remains of a château which crown the heights, are the chief objects of interest at Luz;[1] but

---

[1] This church and château (a little exaggerated in size in M. Doré's illustration) is perhaps the most curious and perfect specimen of a mediæval castle that we shall meet with; its ramparts and loopholes commanding the different points of approach from the neighbouring valleys.

CHÂTEAU NEAR LUZ.

the majority of travellers pay it only a flying visit. The French people prefer St. Sauveur, or Cauterets, for a residence, and tourists make it merely a place for a mid-day halt. In the heat of the day in summer, its principal street is crowded with vehicles stopping at the hotels, with horses and guides and hangers-on of all descriptions; with beggars ad libitum, and with any number of pigs.

We scarcely know how to give an adequate impres-

sion of the importance of the pigs in a place like Luz. They occupy the principal places in the streets and in the doorways of buildings, and the inhabitants seem with one consent to give way to them. In driving into the town we must turn out of the way for fear of disturbing a group that are fast asleep in the middle of the road; and when we alight at our hotel we shall probably find a crowd of loungers superintending the operation of washing them in the stream that flows through the

VIEW AT SUNSET NEAR LUZ.

street, water being poured over them with a large iron ladle as they repose in the sun, submitting placidly to the operation of basting before their time. At Granada, in Spain, every one keeps a pig in the autumn, to fatten for Christmas, and it is considered unlucky not to possess one. The Spanish gentlemen who sit about the doorways here and watch these operations, must be gratified at the adoption of at least one of their customs by the people of Luz.

There is a good carriage-road from Luz to BARÈGES, the distance being about five miles of continual ascent through a somewhat dreary valley, which is often flooded in spring and winter; giving it that forsaken and ruinous appearance, that we see in the valley of the Rhone near Sion.

As we approach Barèges the mountains close in upon us and their sides become more and more barren, the wind blows in gusts, and the air is quite cold in the shade.

The situation of Barèges itself seems at first sight the most uninviting of any in the Pyrenees; even the guide-books

LUZ.

cannot praise it; what Mr. Packe said of it in 1867 is nearly true to-day:—

'The town of Barèges is the sort of place we should expect from the approach, one long street of wretched houses, with a gap at intervals where an avalanche has swept them away and a row of wooden houses has been substituted. Here they sell hardware, cotton-stuffs, and some of the coarser sort of the celebrated woollen Barège shawls, the finer ones being manufactured at Bagnères de Bigorre and Luz.

'The architecture of the town is certainly not imposing, and the climate does not more recommend it. Barèges being at an elevation of 4084 feet above the sea, all the chilly mists of the surrounding mountains here collect, and the wind at times blows down this defile with such violence that for five months in the year the place is uninhabitable. The ground is covered with snow to the depth of fifteen feet, and all the population emigrate except seven or eight of the most hardy, who remain to take care of the houses and furniture, and are kept close prisoners for many weeks.

'The bath establishment is a dreary stone building; sixteen gloomy little cellars, admitting neither air nor light, are set apart for those who can afford the luxury of a private bath, the price

BARÈGES.

of which is one franc, twenty-five cents; and for these there is such a demand that without being registered in the doctor's book you can hardly procure one.'

The waters of Barèges are so much esteemed for their curative properties that the baths are crowded with invalids, and the French administration has established a military hospital here for the treatment of gun-shot wounds, and other injuries.  It is said that as many as

SUMMER VISITORS AT BARÈGES.

ten or twelve thousand persons take the waters during a summer season. The water is disagreeable to the taste and smell, and this, added to the discomforts of a crowded place and a decidedly *triste* situation, do not appear very inviting to a visitor.

But the weather is fine, and warm in the middle of the day, and we find ourselves tolerably comfortable in our mountain lodging, more than 4000 feet above the sea; in the midst of a community of sick men, old women, and decrepit, all huddled together on a ledge of rock, like birds in a nest. The stormy winds that blow down the valley in sudden gusts, and moan in the crevices of the rocks, sound rather drearily, it is true; but what will it be, in a few months' time, when, increased to a hurricane and accompanied with snow, they will sweep away in their winter strength both ' man and his dwelling-place,' and Barèges will have a second season, with another class of visitors who are less fastidious perhaps,

WINTER VISITORS AT BARÈGES.

less infirm, less careful to drink the waters, but otherwise not unimportant, and as certainly to be expected in season as their summer friends.

The presiding deity of Barèges is the 'Pic du Midi de Bigorre.' The inhabitants love, honour, and obey its teaching; they look to it for the signs of the times and seasons, and the sense of its presence is ever near them. In the lonely track over the Tourmalet, and down the valley of the Adour towards Bigorre, it is continually in sight, and by the movements of the clouds round its summit, or by the sharpness of its outline against the sky, the wayfarer is encouraged or cautioned on his route.

Before we leave Barèges we take advantage of a clear day to see the view from the Pic du Midi, which is considered to be unequalled in the Pyrenees, for its extent. Its extraordinary position, standing considerably northward of the central chain, with no mountains of equal height (9439 feet) near it, and its easy approach to the summit, render it more worth ascending than any other of equal height. It takes three hours on foot, and nearly four on horseback. There is a clear path, and no guide is necessary.

We first follow the route leading over the Tourmalet, and then, turning to our left, ascend a shoulder of the mountain until we come to a little lake, and a cabin where it is possible to get a night's lodging. From this point, where we make a short halt, the path leads in a zigzag direction, up the, now steep and barren side, of the Pic, from whence we occasionally obtain distant views of the valley.

The view from the summit, which is at least 1500 feet above the lake, and more than 5000 above Barèges, surpassed all expectation in its grandeur and extent. Our position here was so isolated, that even the vast chain of the Pyrenees, to the south, seemed to be separated from us, and so precipitous were the sides of the Pic du Midi that we scarcely felt as if we were on terra firma. Before us, the solitary Pic de Montaigu, and the plains of France extending into apparently illimitable space, and behind, all the most prominent peaks of the Pyrenees. It was like looking down upon a gigantic map in relief, showing the little towns, the bright green valleys, the dark rocks and the fields of snow. Immediately at our feet there was nothing but rock, but lower down there were slopes of grass, bright with gentian and other wild flowers; the base or frame of this giant mountain being 'cast'—as Mr. Paris calls it—'in a brown micaceous schist, which, cropping out from the surface in masses, sparkles with metallic brilliancy.'[1]

It is difficult to describe, without repetition, the views from these summits, as they must necessarily have so many points of similarity; but the reader may take the word of every one who has had a successful day for the expedition, that there is nothing comparable to it, at the same altitude in the Pyrenees.

As we said before, it is rare to get a clear day for

[1] There is an observatory here with daily telegraphic communication in summer with Bagnères de Bigorre.

these ascents; let us now hear M. Taine's account of one on a cloudy day.

'Départ à quatre heures du matin dans la vapeur. Les pâturages à travers la vapeur ; on voit la vapeur. Le lac à travers la vapeur ; même vue !

'Commencement de l'escarpement ; montée au pas, à la queue l'un de l'autre, chaque cheval ayant le nez contre la queue du précédent, et la queue contre le

nez du suivant, comme au jour de sortie aux collèges d'équitation.

'*Première heure:* Vue du dos de mon guide et de la croupe de son cheval.

'*Deuxième heure:* La vue s'élargit ; j'aperçois l'œil gauche du cheval du guide. Cet œil est borgne, et il ne perd rien !

'*Troisième heure:* La vue s'élargit encore. Vue de deux croupes de cheval et deux vestes de touristes, qui sont à quinze pieds au-dessus de nous. Ils jurent et je jure. Cela nous console un peu.

'*Quatrième heure :* Joie et transports ; le guide me promet, pour la cime, la vue d'une mer de nuages.

'*Arrivée :* Vue de la mer de nuages. Par malheur nous sommes dans un des nuages. Aspect d'un bain de vapeur quand on est dans le bain.

'*Bénéfices :* Rhume de cerveau, rhumatisme aux pieds, lumbago, congélation—bonheur d'un homme qui a fait une ascension !'

Leaving Barèges and its invalids, it is with a certain sense of relief that we find ourselves once more winding slowly up the Bastan valley, on our way to Bigorre.

On a dull, clouded day (which is very frequent here) the pass of the Tourmalet is dreariness itself, and we cannot get rid of the feeling of being half imprisoned by these gloomy, and apparently tottering, walls that rise before us, cold and desolate-looking where avalanches have passed down ; with deep shadows in overhanging places, so like solid, substantial forms that it was difficult, as Miss Edwards expresses it, 'to believe that shadows could be so real—still more difficult to believe that light could be so shadowy.' The little green oases of pasture-land at the valley's base, and the occasional signs of human habitation, seeming only to add to its deserted appearance.

The distance from Barèges to BAGNÈRES DE BIGORRE is twenty-five miles, but the steepness of the ascent, and the time occupied for resting, make it a journey of eight or nine hours.

Our path, which is nearly due eastward, passes between the Pic du Midi and the principal chain of the Pyrenees, the Tourmalet forming the connecting link between the mountains ; and it is not until we reach the col, which takes about two hours and a half, that we get any considerable view, or feel to some extent released from our prison-house.

When we have descended for about an hour, by some very steep and rough zigzags cut in the rock, we get a fine view of the Pic du Midi, and are once more amongst pleasant pastures watered by the river Adour, which here takes its rise and which we follow on its left bank almost all the way to Bagnères de Bigorre.

Another hour's descent, and we meet gaily-dressed people, riding and walking about, who seem to belong to another world (each valley is so shut in and distinct).

and in the little town of Gripp, where we halt, there are carriages that have brought pleasure-parties from Bigorre, whose drivers are clamorous for a 'back fare.'

The situation of Gripp is so picturesque, and the Hôtel des Voyageurs so good and comfortable, that we are unwilling to leave it. Some of our party who have taken up their quarters here for the night in order to start early, by Arreau, for Luchon, where they will await us—have strolled out to visit some beautiful waterfalls in the neighbourhood.[1] Wishing them au revoir, we drive down the valley in the cool of the evening to Bagnères de Bigorre, rattling through the streets of the town after dark, just sufficiently lighted to enable us to see the crowd that is walking up and down a wide 'allée,' shaded by two rows of trees, and bounded on either side by cafés and shops.

Bagnères de Bigorre, built on the left bank of the Adour, is not only one of the most ancient, but it is one of the largest and most prosperous towns in the Pyrenees,[2] having a permanent population of upwards of 9000, besides accommodating in the season 6000 or 7000 visitors. Its situation, neither in the mountains nor in the plains, the cheapness of provisions and other commodities, the moderate rent of houses, the mild saline springs, and the general character of the town for health, combine to recommend it, not only to a large number of valetudinarians, but to that numerous body of English people who reside permanently abroad.

---

[1] This is the best and most direct route to Luchon from Bagnères de Bigorre, over the Hourquette d'Aspin and the Col de Peyresoude (see map). Travellers will find a very comfortable little inn at Arreau, where they can break the journey.

[2] Froissart speaks of it as a 'goodly enclosed town called Bagnères, the inhabitants of which had a hard time of it in 1369, when war broke out between France and England.'

It is a pleasant change to come down again towards the plains and spend a few days quietly in a town, with good inns, bright-looking streets and well-built houses; and curious, to find the English language spoken continually, to hear the click of croquet ('le jeu d'arc,' as the French call it), to see cricket bats, and to be asked in English at the shops if we will buy any 'Pale Ale.' On Sunday morning at the little English church, at the Club, and even in the streets, we might almost fancy ourselves in a country town in England, so familiar and so frequent are the signs of our nationality everywhere.

But if we go into the principal streets on market-days, we shall see a variety of costumes and meet people of many nations. There are itinerant merchants in Spanish costume, with gay silk ribbons, woollen rugs, &c., for sale; and there are rows of shops for the display of woollen goods, which may be bought there much more reasonably than at Eaux-Bonnes or Luchon. An old woman, with a large capulet folded over her head, in a fashion more picturesque than comfortable, one would imagine, offers us ten fine fresh figs for a sou (we have had to pay twice as much for the same at Seville), and young girls with chequered handkerchiefs (made at Pau) tied round their heads, sell flowers and fruit to passers-by.

If we were to go to market this morning, we could purchase ducks, fowls, and turkeys at prices that would make the British householder envious to hear of; and there is an air of plenty and contentment about the place that does one good to witness.

The people that come in from the neighbourhood in such numbers, that in the evening we can hardly force our way through the crowded allée, look prosperous and healthy; and we cannot help contrasting them in our minds, with the inhabitants of other beautiful valleys, such as at Stachelberg in Switzerland, or Tintern on the Wye, in which the people, old and young, are absorbed into unhealthy manufactories and confined all day in close dwellings—where, from the nature of their occupation, the windows are obliged to be kept closed—emerging only in the evening, a long train of pale faces filing off through the rising mist, to return to the mill again before the sun, which only reaches the valley for a few hours, has had time to shine upon them. Happy the people of such valleys as that through which the Adour flows, that they can live and thrive on agricultural labour, and put by for a rainy day, more in one summer month than a Dorsetshire labourer is able to do in a year.

We spend our days rather lazily, and our evenings pleasantly enough at Bagnères de Bigorre; there is no lack of beautiful walks whichever way we turn, and plenty of pleasant English society in the evening, varied, if we please, by balls, concerts, and occasional performances at the theatre.

The walks in the neighbourhood are delightful; you cannot proceed in any direction for half an hour without coming upon some fresh view of the mountains; and if you happen to ascend by the shady paths behind the 'Établissement,' or better, by the east side of the valley, you will be enticed on and on, by the gradual opening of the prospect, until you may find yourself high above the valley when evening closes in.

On one occasion we spent the day on the heights above Bagnères, sketching, and watching the changing aspects of the Pic du Midi, as it every now and then emerged from clouds (which never entirely left it, although it was clear overhead), and were glad of any shade or wood in our path.

As we sat under the trees, there were sounds of voices above our heads, and looking upwards, we discovered men and boys perched up thirty or forty feet high in the air, either on the branches of the trees, or on three poles fixed triangularly in the ground.

Travellers see strange sights; in the Landes there were men literally 'as trees walking;' here they seem to nestle in the branches, and cradle in the wind. They are spreading nets for the wood-pigeons that flock to this neighbourhood in great numbers in the autumn months, and are perched up aloft to throw their nets; the poles and branches bending with their weight, swaying backwards and forwards in the wind, in a manner that appears most dangerous to the uninitiated.

We had been wandering hither and thither, with that uncertainty which is the delight of a mountain ramble; we had come suddenly upon a flock of sheep, and had had a sharp battle with the dogs in charge of them, which are fierce and almost dangerous when attacked; we

had nearly trodden upon a shepherd boy, who lay hidden in the long grass, who had

> ' Fashioned a flute from a willow spray,
> To see if within it the sweet tune lay ;'

and who, careless apparently of his flock, and heedless of us, was repeating some quaint Béarnais air. We had passed up, far above pasture land and trees, and gained a point where, if the eye could have penetrated the atmosphere that alone limited the horizon northward, it seemed as if we might have seen half over France. We were rather late in returning, and by the time we had reached the pastures, and the place where the shepherd boy still lay—gazing lazily into the valley and watching his flock careering down the steep slopes—it was almost dusk.

We sit down to rest for a while—to watch the effect of the sun leaving the highest peaks, whilst Bagnères de Bigorre, several hundred feet below, is disappearing fast from view, and sparkling with little glow-worm lights—when, looking farther down the valley, we see a slowly moving dark line, serpent-like in motion, winding noiselessly through the trees (some monster apparently, attracted by these earth stars), now burrowing underground, and now, as it comes nearer, showing two flaming eyes, and a tail with glittering scales. This monster is a creation of the 'Compagnie du Chemin de Fer du Midi,' and in its sides there are little lighted cells containing atoms of human life. What, we wonder, does the little flute-player, what do all the children of the mountains, think of steam ?

## CHAPTER IX.

### LUCHON.

'Il est convenu que la vie aux eaux est fort poétique, et qu'on y trouve des aventures de toute sorte, surtout des aventures de cœur.

'Il est également convenu qu'aux eaux la conversation est extrêmement spirituelle, qu'on n'y rencontre que des artistes, des hommes supérieurs, des gens du grand monde ; qu'on y prodigue des idées, la grâce et l'élégance, et que la fleur de tous les plaisirs et de toutes les pensées y vient s'épanouir.

'Si la vie aux eaux est un roman, c'est dans les livres. Pour y voir de grands hommes, il faut les apporter reliés en veau, dans sa malle.'—*Taine*.

IN the midst of a broad and fertile valley, with mountain slopes of pasture and wood on either side ; amidst groves of trees, from under banks covered with moss and lichen, burst forth the far-famed springs of LUCHON ; the resort of invalids and 'malades imaginaires,' from the days when Roman emperors drank these waters and Fabia Festa paid her vow to the god Lixon (giving the name of Luchon to the little town built near the rocks, whence the healing waters flowed) —to the present time, when several thousand people throng its streets.

Luchon is the favourite resort of nations both north and south of the Pyrenees ; amongst Parisians it is one of the most popular of 'Les Eaux,' and its fame has reached Madrid, which is deserted in summer time for its waters and fresh breezes. It is now easily reached, either from France or Spain, by railway, and there are, also, several bridle-paths by which it may be approached from the Spanish frontier. The latter are often taken—just as in the hot summer months the modern Florentine, who is stout of heart and strong in the chest, forsakes the dried-up banks of the Arno and the shadow of Giotto's tower, for the bracing air of Switzerland, making his way, as we have seen him, over the snows of the St. Theodule to Zermatt—so do certain brave-hearted Madrileños

come over by the bridle-paths from Jaca, Pantecosa, and the Port de Venasque, and make their sudden appearance on horseback at Luchon.

How shall we describe this shrine—the object of so many summer pilgrimages? Perhaps we cannot do better than compare it, for an instant, with Chamounix, in Savoy, so familiar to most of our readers.

If we can imagine Chamounix, a town consisting of about two hundred hotels and lodging-houses, in the midst of a fertile valley, and surrounded with trees; if

VALLEY OF LUCHON.

we can picture (a stretch of imagination, we admit) a little park outside the town, with trim lawns, beds of flowers, fountains, an artificial lake with gaily-painted boats upon it à la Bois de Boulogne, and a pretty boulevard, lighted by gas at night, with trees at regular intervals; and if we can further picture Chamounix without Mont Blanc, without its glaciers or any ice or snow, and without the bracing air that is born of them; a place where guides are *raræ aves* and knapsacks almost unknown, where guns are fired indeed often enough, not to signalise the ascent of a mountain, but of a fire balloon; where kid gloves are more the *mode* than suits of tweed, and where Frenchmen take the place of Englishmen in native esteem—we get some idea of Luchon.

There is a certain similarity in the two places; they are both the head-quarters from which to make excursions; both are situated on rivers in the midst of a broad valley, with high mountains on each side. There is a drive up to the end of the Vallée du Lys, as to the Col de Balme; and there is a climb, to the Port de Venasque, nearly as steep and precipitous as the Breven, with a view therefrom (see page 203) of the Mont Blanc of the Pyrenees with its snow-fields and glaciers.

The comparative heights, &c., of the two places are thus—but the snow-level is more than 1000 feet higher, in the Pyrenees—

|  | Height above sea-level. | Average height of surrounding mountains. | Average temperature. | Native population about |
|---|---|---|---|---|
| LUCHON .. | 2064 | 8000 | 52° Fahr. | 3000 |
| CHAMOUNIX | 3300 | 11,000 | 37° Fahr. | 3000 |

ENVIRONS OF LUCHON.

The town of Luchon, as far as visitors are concerned, consists chiefly of one long street, the Allée d'Etigny, lined with trees, in which are good hotels, cafés, lodging-houses, and shops. At the upper end is the little park just mentioned, with the Thermal Establishment and a handsome Casino, in front of which is the principal promenade. The lower end of the principal street leads to the old town of Luchon, and to the road down the valley towards Toulouse.

The noise, dust, and bustle in the Allée d'Etigny in the height of the season, when more than a thousand visitors are added to the native population, is extraordinary. There are several roads leading from it, and many chalets and houses dotted about the plain, but as it is the fashion to live in the Allée d'Etigny, the crowd is concentrated on this narrow little slip of land, —whether riding or walking, gossiping or dining, reading or sleeping, day or night, there is hardly any peace upon it.

The scene is a brilliant one on a bright sunny day, with the perpetual movement of the gaily dressed crowds of French and Spanish holiday loungers. There is more local colour and variety here than at Eaux-Bonnes; there are more Spaniards, more red berets and gay sashes, and more striking feminine costumes. The shops are filled with Spanish wools and Parisian goods; signboards are festooned from the trees, and a thousand coloured objects arrest the eye. The middle of the roadway is crowded with carriages and horses; the trappings are gay, of course, and the drivers not the least dandified of the party. The horses or ponies they ride, or drive, are little, lean, attenuated animals, of a breed unknown elsewhere, averaging about fourteen hands high—narrow-chested and stiff-looking like wooden toys, certainly not worth more than 5*l.* apiece. But how they scamper all day up and down this Allée, jingling their little bells, how their drivers shout and crack their whips, asking less and less for a 'course' as the sun goes down, and how popular they are, in spite of the danger to life and limb as they career along, is something almost indescribable.

All this we see at a first glance as we drive at a hand-gallop up the avenue, and with shouts and cracking of whips, turn into the courtyard of one of the hotels. It is situated about the centre of the Allée d'Etigny, in a pleasant little garden, slightly sheltered from the road, and we are fortunate at this time of year in getting good rooms at the back. We are near the stables, and there are fowls and pigeons and peacocks in the courtyard, all favourable to early rising, but almost preferable to the noisy little boulevard.

The hotel is full of visitors, chiefly 'pensionaires,' French, Spaniards, and two or three English, all very merry and sociable, methodical in their habits of early rising, taking baths and exercise, and punctual to a fault in assembling to breakfast at ten, and dinner at half-past six.

We have not been many hours in Luchon when we are besieged with inquiries as to what '*ascensions*' we have made, and it is quite clear that we shall have no peace until we have gone the 'regular round.' But before exploring the environs, or indeed going very far beyond the town, we must see more of the people. The excursions to any great distance, or height, will generally be performed alone; for there is not time to go far between breakfast and dinner, and who could be absent at such times, especially pensionaires, who pay by the day?

It is about eight o'clock on a summer's morning when

we first walk out in Luchon. The mountains look fresh and green from the late rains, little flakes of cloud just touch their tops, and here and there some detached portions float down and nestle amongst the trees, or on projecting slopes of grass, where we can distinguish (through a telescope) sheep grazing, and children gathering wood into the winter chalets.

The streets are full of bathers hurrying to and from the 'Établissement,' and as it is rather too early to see the habitués to perfection, we stroll up the 'Allée des Soupirs,' behind the baths, for a couple of hours, by a steep, smooth path through a wood, towards Super-Bagnères. Every five minutes that we are ascending we get more lovely views of the valley, and of the peaks that rise on every side above Luchon. The town is almost *under* our feet, so precipitous are the sides of the mountain, and we see little of it besides slate-roofs and chimney-pots, with one straight row of tree-tops peeping through the smoke and steam, that rise from the town; and just outside, a gigantic new casino and hotel that is in course of construction in 1880. If we were not bound to see the company to-day, we could well spend all our time in sketching here, or in wandering about Super-Bagnères.

It seems a pity that so little is said in English guide-books about Super-Bagnères; the distance to the cabin at the summit is only five miles, and it is an easy ascent. The beautiful walks through the forests, which M. Doré has sketched for us, and the panoramic view from the summit, taking in the plains of France on one side, and the Maladetta on the other, are well known to those who stay in this valley.

It is now eleven o'clock. Luchon has taken its bath, has drunk the waters, has breakfasted well, and is

SUPER-BAGNÈRES.

prepared to promenade, or to make a *petite excursion ;* let us go into the 'Allée d'Etigny' and see 'the world.' At the windows of the white houses opposite there are Spanish women seated, working, or leaning out upon red cushions, which gives the street quite an Eastern effect. The street is more crowded than ever, and the costumes more brilliant and extravagant than any we have yet seen in the Pyrenees. The general effect of the colours of the figures, on foot and on horseback, is certainly very pretty ; and if some of the ladies' dresses startle us a little by their originality—and if we are rather taken aback by seeing a French gentleman in a suit of scarlet, walking along swinging a child's rattle, or riding a diminutive pony, with his legs nearly reaching to the ground—the *tout ensemble* we must admit to be charming.[1]

Here is a group just starting for a ride, and what, perhaps, strikes us most of all is the size and length of spike of their spurs, the formidable weight of their whips, and the insignificant, meek-looking little animals they are going to mount. Four French gentlemen are about to ride a few miles up the valley, and the concourse to see them start, and the interest taken in the matter, is wonderful. There are perhaps two hundred spectators on foot, and fifty men and boys with horses waiting for hire. These last keep up a constant shouting and cracking with their whips, which irritates the ear like irregular line firing. The start takes half an hour, but the crowd is an admiring one, and in no hurry. One aged cavalier relieves his mind by playing on a horn, another, by dint of spurring and reining in his steed,

---

[1] With the remembrance of the dreary-drab costumes, in which some of our countrywomen travel abroad, we shall be almost converted to the fashions of Luchon.

performs some exciting gambols; whilst the other two, who are younger men, are arranging the thongs of their whips in graceful knots round their bodies. Oh! the costume of young France, the superb top-boots and gilt spurs, the velveteen coat, white waistcoat and scarlet tie, the jockey-cap with a feather in it, and a long white whip; and then the *coup d'œil* when all are mounted, and the crowd gives way to let them pass, the air with which they move slowly by, each cavalier with his elbows well turned outwards and his hand placed bravely on his thigh!

With the departure of the cavalcade the crowd disperses, the majority tending towards the park, or 'English garden;' where, under the shade of the trees, by the aid of sirops and ices, and to the sound of falling water, the next few hours may be dozed away.

It would be almost impossible to give to any one who had not seen the Bois de Boulogne near Paris a just idea of the ingenuity displayed in turning the bed of a mountain valley, covered but a few years since with débris (as seen in the illustration at p. 167), into a promenade and miniature park, with its artificial lake, dainty walks lined with tulip-trees and beds of flowers, real waterfalls imprisoned and turned into 'cascades;' fountains and grottoes, chalets and arbours—all designedly pretty and in order. The little boats that pass to and fro on the lake, trail their awnings to reflect their bright colours in the water; and the Swiss chalets on its banks, and the houses in the town, white with green shutters and red curtains at their windows, are all decorated with an eye to the picturesque.

As the afternoon draws on, there comes an almost continual sound of wheels and horses' feet; the jingle of bells drowns the noise of the cascades, and clouds of dust now roll down the valley, marking the track of the returning stream of carriages.

It is only four o'clock. Why do they return so soon? '*C'est le temps de la promenade.*'

Is it then *all* 'promenade'? But let us follow in the direction of the people that we see assembling on a raised walk near the Établissement, where a brass band is evidently the centre of attraction, and around which the chairs are fast becoming occupied. The gaiety of this afternoon promenade is even more striking than that of the morning, and we are introduced to many fresh varieties of the 'butterfly' species.

How we all wander up and down, and gossip and flirt, and pay no attention to the music, may be easily understood by those who have gone through a course of Horticultural Fêtes in London; but how we dress, how demonstrative and how brilliant we are in this clear bright sunny air, can hardly be conceived at a distance. Nor can we altogether picture to the reader the effect of the Señores and Señoritas who have doffed the charming black mantilla and red camellia in the hair, and come abroad in all the glory of modern Parisian costume; nor the knowing little hats with peacocks' feathers worn by *Parisiennes;* nor the children—children only in size and love for bonbons; nor the Spanish dons in white paletôts and chimney-pot hats; nor the dogs, whose 'paradise of whelping and wagging of tails' is clearly not here, for they also are on good behaviour, and can do neither one nor the other. They are muzzled, wrapped in flannel, and carried in baskets, and generally so clipped and washed, that in appearance they belie their origin. There is a diminutive poodle before us now, by nature 'fluffy,' that some whimsical but unkind master has shorn close and clean, all but his head and his tail—a little atom of a pink body tottering up and down, carrying an enormous shaggy head and equally ponderous tail.

Before five o'clock, the numbers increase to a crowd, and at this fashionable hour the habitués—what in modern slang would be called the 'swells'—make their appearance.

There were two figures who always walked arm-in-arm together, and came on the scene about this time, who were as familiar to us as the rocks and the trees; one a tall Spaniard, faultlessly dressed in a black velvet costume of the time of Charles II., with black silk stockings, shoe-buckles, wide collar, and ruff. His friend, a Frenchman (we presume as a contrast), was the most perfect presentment of the stage Irishman it has ever been our lot to encounter abroad; the intention being to signify a gentleman who was fond of '*le sport*,' and as such he evidently found favour amongst the ladies. These two young gentlemen carried everything before them; they were 'in society,' they knew everybody, and disported themselves in the park every afternoon, to the perfect contentment of Luchon.

There is a good band from Paris, but little attention is paid to the music. It adds, however, to the dramatic effect, and it is difficult to get rid of the idea that the promenade is not the stage of some Italian opera, with all these gay moving figures the performers, the background the scenery to 'Guillaume Tell,' and the audience the group seated on the chairs.

But it is not all gaiety. If we look about us a little we shall see at this time of day numbers of invalids and strangers who occupy the chairs; for, just as the heat of the sun at noon draws forth myriads of insects and atoms of mysterious life, so does this afternoon promenade attract to it visitors that we see at no other time.

Amongst them are the ennuyés—'ennuyés parce qu'ils ont trop de fortune et trop peu de chagrin'—men of middle age, and old, in as great numbers, and put to as great straits in the task of killing time, as may be seen anywhere in Europe. Old and faded dandies, preserved

with the greatest care and made 'youthful for ever' by art, lounging away their days in that difficult time between *déjeuner* and *dîner*, alleviated only by this afternoon promenade, which may bring with it, perchance, a timely little flirtation, or something exciting to read in the 'feuilleton' of the 'Petit Journal,' which is sold to the company for a sou. Curious anomaly of life!—strange indeed that men should wish to kill the hours and not the years; that those who find most difficulty in getting through the day, should above all others dread growing old!

Some of the French women that we meet with at these watering-places, on the contrary, are very merry and industrious; they knit and knit as if for their lives. The family group near us, consisting of *maman* and her four daughters, are shouting with laughter; they are delighted with bonbons and with the gambols of a pet poodle. Their happiness is harmless, and certainly unique, for the majority of the people at Luchon are, truth to tell, suffering from the terrible 'ennui.'

Is this really so? Is it possible that in the midst of beautiful scenery, in a delightful climate, and surrounded with every luxury, we can be weary of existence; or, with so many resources, be at any loss for topics of conversation?

Let us take the testimony of a Frenchman. 'Avancez et écoutez,' says M. Taine, to two people who have just sat down:—

'Le monsieur est arrivé avec entrain; il a souri finement et avec un geste d'inventeur heureux; il a remarqué, qu'il faisait chaud. Les yeux de la dame ont jeté un éclair. Avec un sourire ravissant d'approbation, elle a répondu que c'était vrai.

'Jugez comme ils ont dû se contraindre. Le monsieur a trente ans—il y a douze qu'il sait sa phrase. La dame en a vingt-deux—il y a sept ans qu'elle sait sa phrase. Chacun a fait entendre trois ou quatre mille fois la demande et la réponse. Pourtant ils ont eu l'air d'être intéressés—surpris!'[1]

But the time draws near six o'clock and there is a sound of relief, and up and down the Allée d'Etigny alarm bells are rung as if there was a general conflagration. It is needless to add that Luchon listens with willing ears to the voice of the charmer.

---

[1] A characteristic contrast to the bored young Englishman at Chamounix. 'We were compelled,' he writes home, 'to spend ten days of our time unprofitably at that modern Capua, Chamounix—bargaining for artificial agates, eating heavy dinners, racing to the Montanvert against time, and feeding our imaginations on all sorts of ambitious schemes against the neighbouring passes and peaks.'

After dinner we go again to the Parc, and stroll about amongst the crowd, which is much more numerous and miscellaneous in its character.

The inhabitants of the old town, whom in our gaiety we had altogether forgotten, now join the throng. Groups of peasants—men and women, and hundreds whose occupations are to minister to the various wants of the visitors—now take their evening holiday, and a band of *ouvriers* march, singing through the town.

We all keep to the paths and principal walks, enjoying the cool evening air, and watching the sun's rays as they linger on the peaks on the eastern side of the valley, whilst at Luchon itself it is nearly dusk.

As soon as it is dark the gardens are prettily lighted by gas, fire balloons are sent up, rockets fly about, and dancing *al fresco* is commenced; and it is then, when the mountains are hidden from sight, and there is nothing to remind us of their presence, that we see how perfect is the likeness to the 'Bois de Boulogne' or the 'Champs Elysées.' It is also perfect in its similarity to Paris in the various little out-door amusements, of roundabouts, 'tir au pistolet,' little games of chance, and the various devices for getting rid of small change, for which the Champs Elysées are famous.

To complete the illusion, we pay twopence for a chair, and six sous for '*La Presse*' of yesterday (which has just arrived by the evening post), and listen, as well as we can in the hubbub, to a rather harsh interpretation of some well-known operatic airs, which comes from an elevated wooden kiosk hard by. The shrill discordant sounds of some of the notes we attribute to the dampness of the little wooden house in which, pending the erection of a 'grand casino,' some of the stringed instruments are kept.

But we are not to be left long in meditation, we (visitors) are all, as we said before, essentially dramatic, and have our parts to fill ; if we are good for nothing else, we can buy flowers and sugar-plums as long as our purse holds out, and contribute something for the general good.

We had done our duty this evening—we had bought little books of native costume which were utterly untrue, we had bought red 'berets' which we could not wear, we had steadily refused, and afterwards purchased, nicknacks and bouquets innumerable and inconvenient to carry ; and now, having successfully resisted a demand to pay twice for the same chair, and having lighted a last cigar, would be at peace. But it is not to be. A neat little woman, with a white apron, a shining face, and a white handkerchief round her head, suddenly makes her way through the crowd, and bringing a chair, seats herself close beside us. She has brought with her a small round box, which placed on end makes a table ; it is gaily painted, fitted at the top with a little brass roulette, and lighted with a well-trimmed lamp. With a brief introduction, and the faintest apology for intruding upon 'Monsieur,' she commences conversation ; and in less time than it takes to write it, the whole history and gossip of Luchon, of its distinguished and undistinguished visitors, has been told, and told so well, and the family trials and hopes of 'son mari' and 'les petits enfants,' are so skilfully interwoven into the story, that we find ourselves, unconsciously as it were, in the confidence of this little woman, and could no more put her off with a word, or explain that we hate bonbons and never gamble, than we could cut our best friend.

And now will not Monsieur begin—see, all the wheels are spinning ? The chances are dead against us, of course, but what matters it that the wrong numbers always turn up, what heed of the feigned astonishment on the patient face at our side? Before the light goes out we shall have an empty purse and a pocketful of bonbons, and perhaps have made a home happy.

These games of chance are considered the especial 'fun of the fair,' and every one joins in them. Look at the party of little girls seated in a circle near us, whilst kneeling on the ground before them is a grey-haired mountebank, dressed in half Spanish, half Basque, costume, who is telling them love stories, and enlivening the dull parts with interludes of a little game of chance, which might in the half light be thimble-rigging, but which is innocent enough; and when the band leaves off playing, and there is a general movement homewards, see with what a gentle, courtly grace this knight of other days takes leave of his little friends with an 'au revoir.'

It is now past nine—in half an hour the Parc will be deserted, and at ten, Luchon proper will be in bed. The candles are lit at the 'Hôtel des Bains,' by *Françoise*, whose handsome face and picturesque figure (in local costume) will be remembered by English visitors to Luchon in 1880. 'Everybody likes *Françoise*,' and 'everybody,' as it seems to us, buys her photograph and takes it home. The fact is, however, worth recording that delicate people who have come here for the waters, have cause to be thankful for the kind and thoughtful services of *Françoise;* the last figure in our picture of Bagnères de Luchon.

It is worth while, by way of contrast to all the gaiety that we have just witnessed, to take a walk one day through the old town of Luchon, where shops have lately been built, but in humbler fashion than in the Allée d'Etigny. It is only a few yards down the 'Rue de

Commune,' to the old 'Champ de Mars,' the site of the ancient baths, where there are narrow streets and tottering houses, and where we see half-clad women peeping from dark recesses, and children and pigs wallowing in the mire.

It is quiet here; the people seem listless, hopeless, and quite careless of their gay neighbours, content to exist by the produce of a little field work, and a little begging. The line of demarcation is stronger, and the want of sympathy greater between class and class, than we could have believed possible in so small a place. There is no particular enmity or envy apparently, but carelessness—the carelessness of gaiety on one side, of apathy on the other.[1]

In one point only—the only one we can touch upon, as we, lookers-on, have more to do with their outward aspect than with their social or political life—do they beat their livelier neighbours hollow, they are more 'picturesque;' meaning by that word which we have had to use so often in these pages, something that in all the really pretty groups in the Allée d'Etigny, in all the bright costumes (some of them conceived in the most perfect taste, and with true feeling for colour), has not once been achieved; something, in short, that in nature is everywhere, but which, both in buildings and in the figures about them, no matter of what nation or costume, cannot exist without harmonious contrasts, repose of colour, and a certain amount of age. We hover continually between two extremes—Murillo's dirty beggar-

---

[1] It would be unfair to the inhabitants of these valleys to leave an impression of an utterly forsaken race, for there are evidences of industry and of a certain amount of education amongst the better class of Luchonais, which a paternal government, and the wealth spent annually in this valley, have greatly assisted to develop.

boys playing in the sun, or a fête champêtre on the stage; both having the same set mountain scenery, the former harmonising with it, the latter never.

On one of the hot sultry days that we often experience in this valley, we may visit the large white stone building with the imposing façade, called the 'Établissement,' but we shall find it, although handsomely decorated in the interior, inferior in arrangement to similar establishments at the German Spas; and the odour of the waters, and the close hot smell in its corridors, will soon drive us away. In the upper part of the building there is a model of the Central Pyrenees on a large scale, which gives us from a bird's-eye point of view an excellent idea of the relative position and heights of the mountains; also of the snow-levels, the zones of vegetation, the cascades, lakes, churches, villages, &c. There is also a model on a larger scale of the Cirque de Gavarnie, and in the same room are stuffed specimens of the birds and beasts of the Pyrenees, and a geological collection; occupation for a wet day which will be well spent if we can prevail upon M. Lézat to explain to us his models, a favour extended to few.

The atmosphere is so close and hot sometimes at Luchon, that we can do little in the middle of the day besides sit about in the garden of the hotel looking on to the road, feed the peacocks, and read the one local paper over and over again.

We go out again to the Parc, where 'les élégants, couchés sur les chaises, lisent leur journal et fument superbement leur cigare,' and endeavour to solve the mystery, why the women of all classes are so much more cheery than the men, why we so seldom meet a sad Frenchwoman, why the young ladies never seem tired of discoursing of 'les paysanneries adorables de Georges

'Tout en haut, entre les troncs, brille un pan de ciel bleu ; l'ombre et la lumière se coupent sur la mousse grise comme des dessins de soieries sur un fond de velours.'

Sand,' why their elders are never weary of embroidering, and why nearly every Frenchman we meet bears a decoration, which might be that of the Legion of Honour!

We stroll up one of the paths through the trees behind the 'Établissement,' where the stifling sulphureous air ascends from the vast caverns which undermine the mountain side, and come suddenly upon a French artist, sketching, as we supposed, the valley of Luchon. No, his subject was neither rocks nor trees, neither the distant mountains, nor the sunset in the valley; it was 'Still Life,' an elaborate painting on ivory, of grapes and peaches, silver, and dead birds! A 'pot-boiler,' probably, a work of necessity, and more certain to find a purchaser than sketches of mountains or trees, but all of a piece with this artificial life and atmosphere, of which perhaps the reader has heard enough.

The weather is uncertain, but fine enough for short excursions, so we will be off to-morrow to the Vallée du Lys, bidding farewell to Luchon, where we have seen 'le monde;' le 'monde illustré,' le monde parisien, and, to be truthful chroniclers—le demi-monde.

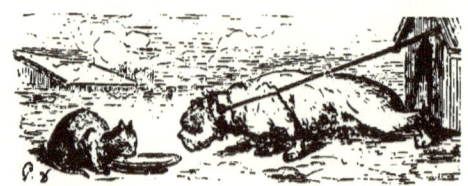

CHAPTER X.

*VALLÉE DU LYS—LAC D'OO—PORT DE VENASQUE.*

THE most popular excursions in the neighbourhood of Luchon are, to the VALLÉE DU LYS; to the LAC D'OO; and to the PORT DE VENASQUE. Either of these may be easily accomplished alone and on foot, without a guide, but we had better speak of them as they are ordinarily undertaken.

The distance from Luchon to the cabin at the end of the Vallée du Lys, where the road terminates, is seven miles, and we have walked it leisurely in about two hours, but on this occasion we are going to drive. Having spoken to the master of the hotel the evening before, he promised to provide us with a carriage for the excursion for twenty-five francs, and a *pour-boire* for the coachman. We remonstrated with him as to the charge, but he referred to the inexorable '*tarif*,' and on further inquiry we found that it was considered quite impossible that two, or three, people could go for less.

The next morning at ten o'clock we found a crowd collected round the gates of the hotel, and a four-horse carriage provided for our expedition. It was an imposing equipage for quiet people; the four thin little horses, with their harness decorated with bright worsted tassels, embroidery, and rows of bells, did not, it is true, look very fresh, and were not thorough-bred; but the driver was a great success, with his white trousers, red sash, black velvet jacket, and scarlet beret, as he sat cracking his long-thonged whip within an inch of his horses' ears that were too much accustomed to it to flinch. We had happily declined the services of a 'guide,' that is, an attendant on horseback to act as an outrider, which our host explained we ought to have, to show us the different points of interest on the road—that it was 'the proper thing to do,' and that, in short, it was considered poor fun to go less gaily.

In England one is accustomed to experience a certain amount of exhilaration when sitting behind four horses careering along a good road, the box-seat on a stage-coach being always considered a privilege; but after two or three summers in the Pyrenees, we venture to think that this pleasure will never be felt so keenly again. The sensation is so frequent here, the teams are so poor and spiritless, the 'ribbons' are so unsatisfactory to handle, and the animals as a rule know so much better than their drivers what to do, that all the pleasure of driving is gone.

We had chosen the excursion to the Vallée du Lys first, because the summit of Mont Signac had had clouds hovering about it for the last three days, which the people at Luchon all say promises rain, and we could easily return, or take refuge in the woods, if overtaken by a storm.

The sun was hot and the sky cloudless overhead, and we were glad to find ourselves going at a good pace, and to feel a slight breeze; but about half a mile on our way we subsided into the faintest of trots, and at

A SUMMER SHOWER

every semblance of a hill, the horses walked, or came to a standstill; the road was dusty, but smooth and excellent, and we put it repeatedly to our 'cocher' whether we might not keep up a trot. It turned out, as it always does turn out in France, that there was a 'règle,' and by that 'règle' he was only to go a certain pace, and, in fact, to make out his day somehow, between Luchon and the Vallée du Lys.

In about half an hour we pass on our left hand the ruins of the 'Castel Viel,' an old tower of defence commanding the valleys and the approaches from Spain; its position is indicated on the promontory behind the town in the middle of the sketch at page 164. It is one of the picturesque 'bits' that no view of Luchon is considered complete without including, and one of the points of interest near which our driver thinks it proper to halt, and to suggest our getting out and paying a visit. We are content to view it from the valley, our only object in a closer inspection would be to see the old woman in charge, whom M. Taine thus immortalises:—

'Il y avait là une vieille mendiante, pieds et bras nus, qui était digne de la montagne. Elle avait pour robe un paquet de lambeaux de toutes couleurs, cousus ensemble, et restait tout le jour accroupie dans la poussière. On aurait pu compter les muscles et les tendons de ses membres; le soleil avait desséché sa chair et roussi sa peau; elle ressemblait au roc contre lequel elle était assise. Si un sculpteur eût voulu faire la statue de la Sécheresse, le modèle était là.'

Continuing up the valley—by an easy ascent on a good smooth road, which our four steeds take at such a deliberate pace that we have time to wander by the road-side and gather the beautiful wild flowers that cluster everywhere, set in a background of delicate ferns and mosses in the crevices of the cool grey rocks—we get easily and pleasantly over the first few miles, when, without any notice or remark, our sleepy driver suddenly turns out of the road, and comes to a dead stop. We protest, but in vain, that we should prefer to continue our journey.

'C'est ici la cascade, Monsieur ; tout le monde s'arrête, voir les eaux.'

It was useless to object that we had already seen cascades enough to last a lifetime, including the 'Cascades des Demoiselles,' the 'Cascade des Parisiennes,' the 'Cascade de la Lune,' and that we were now going to see the 'Cascade d'Enfer'—the driver and the horses were fast asleep, and there was nothing for it but to get out and go through the ordinary routine.

On the left of the road there was a little pathway that led to the cascade, and we could distinctly hear the sound of a waterfall, where the bed of the valley contracted, and the Gave had forced its way through the rocks, on its passage downwards.

We were not permitted to see the cascade alone, for an old cantonnier (that we had seen breaking stones by the road-side) soon made his appearance, and explained that he was the appointed showman, and that no one could safely approach the rocks without his assistance. We knew that we represented 'a tip,' and were prepared to give it to the old man on our return, but preferred seeing this (as all other sights whatsoever) unattended by any showman. The old man assented sullenly, and the foremost of our party, following the path to the waterfall, stepped on to the edge of the rocks, which were smooth and covered with spray. In an instant he went down, as if levelled by a rifle from an enemy in ambush, and slid down to the brink of the fall. The remainder of the party who followed him, as soon as they got upon the rocks, lost their foothold, and could neither advance nor retreat without help from the old cantonnier. These rocks, worn smooth by the water, have a peculiarly slippery and greasy surface, more difficult to tread than any glacier, and affording no sort of foothold.

The barefooted old man conducted us all to terra firma, and we soon regained our carriage; having seen a rather ordinary waterfall, having achieved a series of tumbles, and contributed the worth of about two days' pay to the cantonnier.

But it is as well to remember that a guide is necessary in visiting this waterfall; a fatal accident happened here in 1880, one Achille Durat, a visitor at Luchon, slipped into the chasm, and was dashed to pieces against the rocks below. A stone cross marks the spot where he fell.

Another instalment of the drive, now crossing to the right bank of the river, through woods of beech and hazel, and we come, in about two hours from leaving Luchon, to an open space of pasture-land, where the Vallée du Lys terminates, almost as abruptly as the valley of Leük, near the pass of the Gemmi.

We now leave the road, and proceed to see more waterfalls. Not many yards from the little cabane where a halt is made, we arrive at the foot of the principal fall, the 'Cascade d'Enfer,' where, through a perpendicular fissure in the slate rock, the water descends, throwing clouds of spray which almost hide its base, keeping the vegetation near it in a perpetual summer shower.

We can see far above us amongst the trees, the paths which lead to the upper part of the fall, and on a dizzy height, a stone bridge which spans it several hundred feet above, and we can also see through the trees on which the sun is shining brilliantly, little bright objects, which at first sight might be the prismatic colours reflected by the sun shining on the falling water; but which really have more the appearance (so brilliant are they, and so fitful in motion) of coloured lights, playing through painted windows, on a cathedral pavement.

We soon discover that they are the costumes of equestrians, who are here before us, and who are slowly winding in and out amongst the trees; we are not long in overtaking them, and in being disabused of all romance about the matter. The path is so narrow that one man on horseback more than fills it, and pedestrians are forced to clamber up the rocks to make way for those who are coming down. There must be twenty or thirty of them, including guides, all more or less gaily clad, and all with long whips, which get entangled in the trees. The effect of these processions, viewed from either above or below (an effect we so seldom get in real life), is worth a moment's notice, especially where for a few yards the path is broader, and we see people riding two abreast. There is so much that is suggestive and pleasing in the varied colours, and the grace of their approaching lines, seen half in shadow, half in sunlight, amongst the trees; and much, indeed, that is novel in effect, for how few of us ever have an opportunity of seeing a really picturesque cavalcade, without the element of war or the tinsel of the stage!

We may ascend for upwards of two hours, obtaining different views of the cascade and of the valley—notably that from the bridge that spans the Cascade d'Enfer —until we reach the 'source,' a much sterner scene, where the glaciers of the Crabioules raise their cold, rigid outlines against the sky.

Through the trees, as we returned, we obtained many beautiful peeps far down into the Vallée du Lys, and after passing the second wooden bridge over the falls we left the path altogether, and scrambled down the steep mountain side on a track where timber had been felled, and there was a clearing. We now got into a cloud, which had been gathering for the last hour almost unperceived, and before we reached the cabin were nearly wet through with the rain and mist that enveloped everything.

On our way down we had seen smoke curling through the trees, and knew that there must be a good fire somewhere, but when we went into the cabin to dry our clothes, there was none to be seen. At the spot where we knew there was a fireplace two hours ago, there stood, or rather crouched, four or five Frenchmen, all wedged close together, and facing us—a row of human ornaments in high relief. For some minutes no one moved and nothing was said, until at last one of the five commenced a dissertation on rheumatism, and the dangers of the *colique;* and there gradually rose up such a damp odour from these baking Frenchmen that we were glad to retire. The rain was now pouring down, and the clouds shut out all view, so we hurried into our carriage, and were driven home in less than half an hour, passing groups of drenched equestrians in full retreat. The morning had been so fine that an unusual number of visitors had gone up the valley; great therefore was the havoc amongst the costumes, and all-absorbing the interest at the 'table d'hôte' in the adventures of the day. It was the nearest approach to an excitement that we had yet experienced at Luchon.

For the next twenty-four hours we had a steady cold rain, with a curtain of clouds and mist in front of our windows, penetrating many of the frail wooden dwellings, and rendering them anything but favourable, one would think, to the cure of rheumatism for which Luchon is so famous.

We have said little about the flowers in the Vallée du Lys, for our journey was in the autumn time; but in spring and in early summer this valley is a garden of flowers. In the month of June, as the narcissus fades in the meadows its place is taken by a beautiful pure white lily, about two feet high, with a blossom like the garden lily but smaller and more transparent; its botanic name is *Anthericum liliastrum.* This plant grows in profusion in two or three protected valleys, and in early summer visitors return home laden with bunches picked by

O

women and children. The name of the Vallée du Lys may well be derived from this lily, which is one of the most beautiful flowers in the Pyrenees.

On the third day the rain ceased, but although cloudy, was considered fine enough for a visit to the Lac d'Oo, and to see the cascades. This time nearly all the visitors making the excursion were either English or Germans, and we got off in a rather more undemonstrative manner. The tariff to the Lac d'Oo was twenty-five francs for a carriage with two horses, but our attentive host engaged to get us a pony carriage that would take two persons as far as the Cabanes d'Astau, if we would undertake to drive.

Leaving Luchon by the 'Allée des Soupirs,' on the road to Arreau, we drove through the valley of Larboust, past several small villages (and a little chapel, an object of great veneration by the inhabitants, dedicated to the martyr St. Aventin), until we came to the village of Casaux, where a sign-post directed us to leave the high road to Arreau and Bagnères de Bigorre, and turn off to the left, now in an almost southerly direction, into a path like the strip of a ploughed field.

The horses paid little attention to their driver (being accustomed to look after themselves), but trotted on when they could get a flat piece, climbed over mounds, slid down into large mud pools, stumbled over great lumps of rock, squeezed their way through brambles and brushwood, dragging the light carriage on four wheels up after them 'somehow,' until they came to the village of Oo, consisting of two rows of low houses, between which we had to pass; a narrow and steep stony street, dark, with low roofs overhanging. In front of a door of one of the houses, which seemed to be filled with manure, and from which the most unpleasant odours issued, our horses came to a dead stop. Our monopoly of the entire high street of Oo created no excitement amongst the poor, listless inhabitants, who were too much accustomed to such inroads. The street was so narrow that no one could get out of the carriage excepting into a window, and in front it appeared so much narrower, that we might have given up all progress as hopeless; but what has been done once, can be done again by a French horse, so with a little persuasion, and the cry '*En route!*' which is understood better than any other interjection, we again jolt and heave over stones and loose obstructions, grazing both sides of the street at once, and sinking into mire, over axle-trees and up to saddle-girths.

Through a dirty little hamlet, past one old castle on the heights which we could just see through the clouds, round the steep side of the mountain, by waterfalls, through woods and lanes shaded with beech and ash trees, and on paths that Mr. Packe says 'may *just* be taken in a carriage,' and which Murray describes as 'a very narrow and stony horsepath;'[1] we arrive in about two hours at the 'Granges d'Astau,' where the valley is wider, covered with coarse pasture, and strewn with rocks and stones (the bed probably of some glacier in former ages), terminating in a steep ascent to the Lac d'Oo. Here everything on wheels *must* stop, and those who are unfortunately unable to walk, must wait for their friends' return, or be carried up by 'chaise à porteur' at an angle of 45 degrees or thereabouts.

There are several parties on the way before us, and at least twenty people on foot going and returning from the Lake.

---

[1] This road has been widened and improved during the last few years; but it is still very bad in parts.

On our journey to the Vallée du Lys we said something about the picturesque effect of processions of tourists on the mountains; M. Doré, in the next illustration, has pictured something much more prosaic.

Parts of the pathway were steep and slippery, the

cascades, swelled with the late rains, overflowing the path, which was covered with small streams nearly the whole way up. The sun now shone brilliantly against the polished surface of the rocks, and when we arrived at the Lake the heat seemed extraordinary, at a height of 4900 feet above the level of the sea.

The Lac d'Oo is completely shut in by mountains, excepting at the narrow outlet to the north by which we approach. The water is cold and clear, and reflects on its still surface the lines of the rocks and the cascade at the upper end, which falls into it from the frozen lakes and glaciers above, at a height of more than 800 feet. This extraordinary mountain lake is half a mile in length, and nearly 300 feet deep, and is so deeply set in the mountains that the sun scarcely ever shines on its surface. The view from the cabin on its banks is so varied—with the changing effects of light and shade on the snow-clad summits at sunset and by moonlight—that no adequate idea of its beauties can be obtained, without staying here for a few days, when the weather is settled and clear.

LAC D'OO.

Two or three beds are made up at the 'cabane,' which are to be had by any one who desires to stay, being seldom occupied, excepting by those who make this their starting-point for excursions to the glaciers, and to another 'series of lakes' yet far above us. But the weather is so uncertain in the Pyrenees, that many have been here over and over again, without seeing across this lake, and have had to give up all idea of exploring the snow-slopes, or reaching the Lac Glacé, the last of the upper lakes, 8760 feet above the sea. Mr. Packe enumerates, amongst other attractions of this unique spot, that botanists may find upwards of one hundred varieties of plants in the neighbourhood of the Lac d'Oo.

Before we left the lake it was overshadowed with clouds, and the sides of the mountains were hidden to within a few feet of the water. There was no chance of seeing any effect of sunset, and indeed it was hardly safe to linger so late, as the road home, after dark, would have been quite impracticable.

## Port de Venasque.

The journey to the Port de Venasque and the Port de Picade is a longer one, occupying usually ten or eleven hours. We left Luchon soon after seven A.M., taking the same light pony carriage as to the Lac d'Oo (the late rains having rendered the road to the Hospice very bad, in fact almost impassable), but, this time, having a boy with us to take charge of it during the greater part of the day. The road only extends as far as the Hospice de Luchon, a distance of six miles and a half; for the first mile or two in the same direction as to the Vallée du Lys, past the Castel Vieil, then turning up a gorge in a south-easterly direction, by a steep road through a wood, until we come again into open ground where the Hospice is situated—a large low building, affording shelter, and rough accommodation, for those who need it on their passage to and from Spain ; a dirty, snug, smuggling-looking dwelling, the head-quarters of all kinds of expeditions, hunting, shooting, pedestrian, and contraband.

Here we left the carriage to wait our return ; and crossing the river Pique (now quite a narrow stream) by a bridge a little below on the right, we got to work at once, and commenced the wild ascent of the Port de Venasque. From the Hospice we could see our route winding up, in irregular zigzags, several thousand feet above, just visible here and there, as it rounded a promontory, or when a string of laden mules, that were ascending before us, turned the sharp corners and appeared for an instant on the extreme overhanging edge of the mountain side. The path, which led by a more gentle ascent through woods and over green pastures, immediately in front of the Hospice, was the route to the Porte de Picade ; another and more circuitous route into Spain, by which we shall return.

For the first half-hour after leaving the Hospice, we walk over grassy slopes, keeping well under the shadow of the rocks, but are soon obliged to emerge upon the more exposed part of the path, where the sun's rays are so powerful that, if we had had a guide, we should have been glad to have given him our coats to carry.

As we get higher, still keeping in sight of the Hospice, the air becomes more rarefied, and we are surprised to find a wind. The path is one continual ascent, winding up and up without a break, or scarcely an unexposed position on the side of the rock, and we can now easily understand the danger of this pass in stormy weather, and almost believe in the pathetic story of the fate of nine tinkers, who are said to have been carried down by an avalanche. After reaching a spot where we halt for a few minutes by the banks of five little blue lakes that we find nestling in the mountain side, close to our path, the work begins in earnest, and it would be safer for

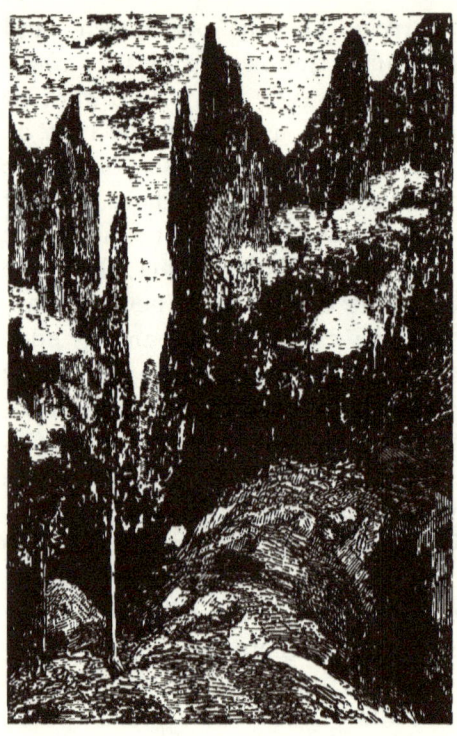

every one to trust to his own feet. The way, so far, has been one that could easily be taken on horseback in favourable weather, but as we near the summit it is nothing but a steep shelving path, cut in the wall of rock, narrow and slippery, covered with loose shale, and here and there some snow. We have to keep quite close to the rocks to get any foot-hold, and can at times scarcely hear each other's voices for a rushing sound, like falling water, but which is only the wind amongst the pines.

We have lost sight of the Hospice for half an hour, and can see neither where we came from nor whither we are tending. At every turn of the zigzag path the wind becomes more powerful, and it is necessary to make a steady stand against each gust as it sweeps down, bringing with it a shower of small stones, which strike against our face as sharp and cold as hail; and thus on we plod, with the bright blue sky above, and clouds and the four little lakes apparently still close to our feet; when suddenly a door opens in the great wall of rock, and we are ushered into Spain by the wind!

The view that has suddenly burst upon us is so magnificent from this elevation, that in spite of the hurricane (for it is here no less, although it is a calm, sultry day in the valley), we steady ourselves by joining hands, and stand in the *Brèche*. The Maladetta, that we have shown in the illustration on p. 203, taken from a spot not far below, is the prominent feature, surrounded by the grandest ranges of the central Pyrenees. The intervening valley is desolate-looking, a sort of 'no-man's land'—Spanish soil, indeed, but territory which no Spaniard is likely to take the trouble to dispute possession of.

There is one solitary hut that we see below, with just sufficient accommodation to shelter a passer-by, but scarcely to give him a night's lodging with a chance of rest; for the rafters are loose, and the hay that formed a bed for some of our friends (who spent the night here when on an expedition to ascend the Maladetta) was nearly blown away when we last visited it.  On the calmest, brightest day in summer there comes up the dark valley on our right hand, that leads to Venasque, a cold and bitter wind—a wind that those who have once felt never forget—the same that haunts the capital of Spain, and sweeps in chilling gusts through the corridors of the Palace at Madrid.

M. Doré's drawing of the Maladetta is almost photographic in its truth and accuracy of outline; also in giving the sterile desolate aspect of the intervening valley, a scene which has been described by many pens but by few pencils.  Its isolated position—and the extent of glaciers and snow-fields, that we can see to best advantage from a point a little above the 'Port' where we attain an elevation of upwards of 8000 feet—give the Maladetta an appearance of height that is quite illusory, and the reader who is only familiar with Swiss mountains may be surprised to learn that the highest peak, the 'Pic de Nethou' (the one on the left in the illustration), is only 11,168 feet above the sea.

Leaving this scene of dreary magnificence, we descend to the cabin (shown in the illustration, p. 204), and making a short halt to despatch a bottle of excellent Malaga wine, we continue our journey, in an easterly direction, keeping close to the spur, or ridge, dividing France and Spain, having the Maladetta on our right hand.

On looking back, we can see with our glass far down into the valley leading to Venasque, and distinguish one or two bright moving specks, which prove to be a party of Spaniards on their way to Luchon; having sent their families and luggage, by a détour of several hundred miles, by railway by Perpignan and Toulouse.  They do

THE MALADETTA

not halt at the cabin, but moving slowly up to the door of rock shown in the sketch, silently disappear.

Nothing can be more extraordinary than the contrast between the French and the Spanish side of the Port de Venasque; the latter (called the Peña Blanca, or white rock) shelving up to the serrated ridge of a sheer precipice on the north side.

THE PORT DE VENASQUE, FROM THE SOUTH.

Continuing our route, over rocks and loose boulders and patches of coarse grass, we pass a few huts for shelter for cattle, and meet a number of baggage-mules on their way to Spain, with their drivers in picturesque rags—each furnished with a red sash, and generally a pistol or a knife in his belt—and in about half an hour reach the Port de Picade, where we obtain an altogether different view, looking towards the Catalonian mountains, which is in many respects finer, and more varied, than that from the Port de Venasque. We now re-enter France, and, by a comparatively easy descent, reach the pastures which lead to the Hospice de Luchon.

Here we make another halt, to wait for some of our party who have been ascending the Entécade, a mountain-peak to the eastward, to which it is not easy to make out the path, without the assistance of a shepherd as a guide. The following note of this walk was made later in the year, on a fine October day :—

'On the Entécade you are in the centre of a magic circle of mountains ; on the east towers the Maladetta, at least four miles distant, yet seeming but a rifle-shot away, so clearly distinguishable is every crevice and contour. From this point of view, the Maladetta appears even more majestic than from the Port de Venasque, owing perhaps to the greater number of lesser peaks with which it challenges comparison. At the foot of the frontier range, of which the Entécade forms part, runs the Garonne, its course marked by several little Spanish villages, dotted in the green landscape.'

Leaving the open pastures and descending rapidly through a wood, rattling down with a hundred goats at our heels, keeping well to windward of them as a matter of prudence, we arrive again at the Hospice just as the sun's rays are leaving the valley, and the old man and the fowls are going to roost.

It takes some time to find our 'cocher' (who has been enjoying a long nap under the trees) and to get the horses put to, but once started we make up for lost time. The two hind wheels of our little basket carriage are closely locked, the whip is cracked until the lash has a large tuft at the end and will crack no more, and all the izards, foxes and bears (if there are any) are put on the 'qui vive ;' the reins are thrown loosely over the backs of our two little lean coursers, and away we go—winding down the side of the valley on the smooth steep road with the

silent swiftness of sleighing, the gay trappings and the fox-tails at the horses' heads flying in the wind, and the bells jingling merrily. We nearly knock over one or two peasants with laden mules, and once are nearly overturned ourselves, but are so near the ground, and leaning back so comfortably in our little land sleigh, that we would not slacken pace for the world; and thus glide into Luchon a little after dusk, having made a run of seven knots in about half an hour.

And so we end our mountain journeys as we began them, riding and driving where, according to the muscular theory, we ought to have been on foot, enjoying these excursions much more (to our shame be it spoken) for the little spurt at the beginning and the end.

There are many other walks, and rides, in the neighbourhood of Luchon, of which we should like to speak, but space will not permit; moreover, we are reminded by our French friends that we have done all that is expected of us, and may rest content—that, in short, we may enjoy the 'bonheur d'un homme qui a fait une ascension,' and repose in peace after the labours of the climb.

## CHAPTER XI.

### ST. BERTRAND DE COMMINGES—TOULOUSE.

BEFORE we left Luchon, the weather began to give unmistakable signs of breaking up, the clouds came down and took possession of the valley, the rain put out the gas illuminations, and the fire-balloons would no longer go up. It was the end of August, the 'season' was nearly over, and great was the rush to get places in the diligences for Montrejeau. We had taken them a week in advance, or we should have had difficulty in getting away, as carriages were also at a premium; and when our time came we found our diligence loaded, and literally crammed, in every corner.[1]

It rained hard as we went swaying from side to side down the valley, the mountains hidden from sight, the fields fast becoming lakes again, and sprouting with a sudden growth of huge umbrellas, where the women were gathering their last crop of Indian corn.

About ten miles from Luchon, we join the valley of the Garonne; the same river that we passed over at Bordeaux, broad and wide, laden with ships, and afterwards saw at the 'Port de Picade,' a narrow thread of water winding through the Val d'Aran. We are on the high road to TOULOUSE, but make a halt at Comminges

---

[1] Travellers now leave Luchon easily by railway, and in their rapid flight down the valley, of course, miss much of its picturesqueness.

THE VALLEY AFTER RAIN.

to examine one of the most interesting relics of ancient architecture that we shall see in our travels.

On the left hand of the road to Montrejeau, near the Loures railway station, seventeen miles from Luchon, on a rocky promontory (said to be the site of the ancient Lugdunum Convenarum founded by Pompey the Great

B.C. 66), stands the beautiful Gothic church of St. Bertrand de Comminges, founded in the twelfth century. The interior is rich in sculpture, carved woodwork and stained glass; there are monuments to the memory of ecclesiastical dignitaries, and notably a marble tomb (1352) to the memory of Bishop Hugh de Castellione. In the choir is a wooden box behind a grating, containing the bones of Saint Bertrand *'très degradés'*; and hanging from the wall under the tower is a crocodile supposed to have been brought from the Crusades.

The town, once a large one, contains only a few hundred inhabitants; but our interests are more with the dead than the living at Comminges, and we are occupied nearly the whole of the day in tracing the Romanesque ruins both in the cloisters of the church and in the precincts of the town, where there are the remains of an amphitheatre, and parts of the Roman wall which once enclosed the town, with the wolf of Romulus over one of the gates.

There are other antiquities in the neighbourhood of St. Bertrand: there is the grotto of Gargas on the mountain side, which we see in the direction of Bigorre, also the fine Romanesque church of St. Just, with columns from an old temple built into its structure.

The illustration will give some idea of the position of Comminges and its cathedral, and of the importance of

ST. BERTRAND DE COMMINGES.

this position to the ancients in time of war. The height of the promontory and the towers of the church are exaggerated in M. Doré's drawing; but the sketch will serve its purpose if it causes travellers to stop here (if only for an hour) on the journey from Luchon to Toulouse or Bigorre.

Leaving St. Bertrand de Comminges, and crossing the Garonne, we soon arrive at Montrejeau, and, still following the course of the Garonne, go by train to TOULOUSE. Montrejeau, now the railway junction, was for many years the terminus of the railway system southwards, a temporary wooden shed, where in all weathers, and at all times of day, or night, travellers have been stranded, to wait their turn for the diligences, and have had to put up with the shelter which the wooden shed afforded, or the not much better accommodation to be found in the old town. What travellers have suffered here during the many years that the railway stopped abruptly at Montrejeau, will never be known, or much cared for, by those who roll easily past it in express trains from Toulouse to Bigorre.

The train takes us in less than three hours to Toulouse, and we are soon installed in comfortable quarters in an Hôtel, with rooms looking on the 'Place du Capitole,' a large open square in the centre of the town, with rows of shops and arcades, and on one side the Hôtel de Ville.

Early in the morning we are awakened by a sound which to our sleepy senses might be the working of an enormous hive, or the murmuring of the sea upon the shore; and on looking out we find the whole 'Place' (nearly as large as the Palais Royal) covered with umbrellas of various shapes and colours, and a crowd of people running in and out from under them, like rabbits in a warren. It is market morning and it has been raining in the night, and the people are now drying their enormous umbrellas in the sun. There are nearly a thousand people who have come in from the country round with provisions of all kinds, which are both cheap and plentiful. Their costume differs very little from what we see in other parts of France, though the flower-girls are more robust than those of Les Halles, and the patois is less easy to understand than Parisian French. There is a certain statuesque grace about the attitude of many of the women, which their simple costume, their bronzed complexion (and the white, or coloured, handkerchiefs which they wear round the head), render very picturesque; but the hardships of field life and exposure to the weather gives them a hard, aged appearance before they are twenty. Many of them have walked ten miles to the market in the rain, and will return along a dusty road, to work again in the fields and to sleep in a hovel with cattle. The market seems almost entirely conducted by women, and there is a ceaseless clamour of voices up to a certain hour in the morning, when both market and market-women disappear.

It is pleasant to see the Toulousaines, with their fresh bright faces and white caps, going to church and to market, in the early morning, and strange to see the capacity of their baskets and the prices that they give for provisions in this favoured land. Our host, who, it is fair to say, is celebrated for keeping the best table in Toulouse, is purchasing baskets of fruit at what, were we to divulge the secret, would be considered fabulous prices; and which make one wonder that half the produce of Languedoc is not sent, in spite of the octroi, straight by train to 'Les Halles,' for the benefit of Parisians with short purses.

We spoke of the pretty women of Toulouse; let a French writer describe them a little more minutely:—

'Les Toulousaines sont en général petites, et, quoiqu'elles aient les cheveux noirs, la blancheur de leur teint ne peut être surpassée. Dans leurs traits, le piquant s'unit à la grâce ; la fraîcheur de leur visage, l'incarnat de leurs lèvres attestent la pureté du sang ; des dents petites et perlées, des yeux superbes, presque toujours fendus en amande et voilés par de longues paupières, ajoutent à leurs agréments. A ces qualités extérieures, elles joignent une âme aimante et un caractère d'une pétulance singulière ; elles sont franches, communicatives et gaies.' And, we should add one more trait, which is too patent to leave unnoticed, which the Abbé le Voisvenon shall tell for us. 'Ce peuple, le plus spirituel de la terre, a un tort immense à mes yeux : ils ne se lavent pas assez les mains.'

Toulouse has an increasing population of 132,000, and now ranks as the 'seventh city of France.' Its buildings are for the most part poor and built of brick, its streets are long, narrow, irregular, and very badly paved. There is one fine site in the town, the 'Place du Capitole,' of which we have spoken, spacious and central, and from which most of the principal thoroughfares diverge ; and one distant view of the mountains to be obtained, in clear weather.

A great number of visitors pass annually through Toulouse, owing to its central position, and to its being one of the highways to the Pyrenees.

The churches of most interest are those of St. Sernin and St. Etienne. The illustration on the next page gives an accurate idea of the picturesque proportions of St. Sernin, with its beautiful octagonal tower with five tiers of arches, its semicircular east end, and its graceful porches. Its date is partly of the eleventh, and partly of the fourteenth, century, and although the largest church in Toulouse, it is built of brick.

ST. SERNIN.

There is some curious wood-carving in the interior; in the side chapels and crypt there are some remarkable relics, and a model showing the position of the church before the Revolution, when it was fortified, and surrounded with walls, like the church of the Templars we have seen at Luz. The size of the interior and the length of the nave, redeem it from insignificance, but so much has been added and altered since the time of building, that the interior and exterior of St. Sernin have the appearance of being different and distinct edifices.

At the opposite side of the town, at the end of an open Place, but built up against by houses on each side, is St. Etienne, the Cathedral of Toulouse, of which we can get no favourable view, or comprehend

very clearly the designs of its various architects. There is a nave of the thirteenth century half-finished in the sixteenth, a clock tower of another period, and a choir

TOULOUSE.

(flamboyant) of another. The tower is irregular in its sides, the rose-window is not in the centre of the nave, and the choir does not appear to belong to the rest of the structure. The whole building is a confusion of styles, and a distinct example of none, but the interior (like that of St. Sernin) is imposing from its size and height, and in the choir there is some fine stained glass.

In both these churches we could not but notice the simple and quiet (not to say slovenly) manner in which the services were conducted; the neglected state of many of the chapels, and the generally uncared-for appearance of the interiors. We remember seeing a little bundle carried in on a cushion, which was a living child, and another bundle hurried out, which was dead; and we can just carry away in our memories the figures of a few men and women kneeling in the half-light, and the monotony of the 'ora pro nobis,' but there was little brightness, gilding, or display of any kind, and scarcely anything to remind us that we were in a land 'where tapers burn all day for departed souls.'

Toulouse, the capital of the department of the Haute Garonne, situated in the centre of a thriving province, with its 'Canal du Midi,' and its river and railway communication, both with Marseilles and Bordeaux, is admirably placed for commerce, and the plains of Languedoc are sufficiently fruitful to supply its inhabitants cheaply and plentifully all through the year. It has little appearance of activity or enterprise, compared with other cities of the same size and commercial importance, but rather the aspect of a city that is content to live on its ancient reputation. Not many years ago the town and people of Toulouse were thus epigrammatically described:—

'Petites gens, petit commerce, rues étroites, esprits plus étroits que les rues, prétentions monumentales et résultats microscopiques, mélomanie suspecte, amour effréné des histrions, pratique du culte réligieux à la manière un peu idolatrique—voilà Toulouse.'

Its history dates back thirteen hundred years, its judicial rights and privileges are recorded through many centuries, and the statues of its worthies in the 'Salle des Illustrés,' in the Hôtel de Ville, form an imposing array. In this gallery we are led through a series of historic recollections, we are reminded of the days of the Romans, and of the more romantic troubadours (who are still kept in remembrance in Toulouse by the 'Société des Jeux Floraux'), and are brought by a chain of events, more or less connected with our own countrymen and their brave deeds, to the peaceful, but not unimportant event, the construction of the Canal du Midi in the time of Louis XIV., by Riquet, an engineer. This canal, which brought so much prosperity to Toulouse and to the inhabitants of the plains of Languedoc, is celebrated in local song, and the name of Riquet is held in grateful remembrance. It was a colossal undertaking, uniting the two seas of the Mediterranean and the Bay of Biscay, being 150 miles long, and constructed for barges of 100 tons burden. The railway has almost superseded its use, but the peasantry still sing:—

> 'Ce que toujours le monde admire, âge en âge,
>   Ce que le Languedoc contemple avec amour,
> Et qui fait le bien-être à la ville au village :
>   C'est la canal de Riquetou.
> Oui, grâces à Riquet, la cité de Toulouse
> D'aucune autre n'est jalouse.'

\*    \*    \*    \*    \*

Riquet was not a native of Toulouse, but of that the

poets take little heed: his statue is placed amongst the worthies in the Salle des Illustrés, and he is remembered by a grateful province.

We have left the most interesting building in Toulouse until the last. In a narrow street called the Rue des Arts, in the cloisters of a desecrated church of the Augustines, there is an admirable collection of busts and casts from the antique, statues, marbles, and Roman remains. An idea of the general arrangement may be gathered from the next illustration, but the extent of it, and the almost numberless fragments of sculpture that have been collected together—especially from the valleys of the Pyrenees, and the banks of the Garonne—could hardly be imagined. It is considered the finest provincial collection in the South of Europe, from the variety and excellent preservation of the antiques, and from the careful manner in which they have been classified and arranged, 'to form an uninterrupted chain in the history of Art from the Gallo-Roman period to the Renaissance.'

It is impossible to walk round these cloisters, even in the most cursory manner, without being struck with the character portrayed in many of the busts, with the beauty of the friezes (the originals of many that are familiar in our modern schools of Art), and the chaste vigorous designs of the Roman sculptors. In such perfect preservation are some of the architectural remains, and so marked is the individuality of many of the busts, that we are brought face to face as it were with both the authors and their works, with the startling effect of a discovery at Pompeii.

We are permitted to examine this collection at leisure, to copy some of the friezes, and to sketch the courtyard in the centre, where, through the Gothic arches, we can

CLOISTERS AT THE MUSÉE

see the sun shining upon the tower of the desecrated church, and upon the trees in the courtyard which twine their branches round the marble pillars, and half hide the remains of statues and votive altars lying in the long grass. We stay until evening, and are finally swept out by the custodian with the dust of ages, and some little bits of sculptured stone, that the curators of the British Museum would not despise.

There is a gallery of modern paintings upstairs (the room in which they are hung being part of the interior of the church) that we are bound to see; but in the whole collection there are few pictures that one would care to possess, or which call for notice. They are for the most part inferior copies of the old masters, and some modern works chiefly by French provincial artists. There are enormous canvases covered with allegories, and religious subjects are also numerous; but if it be true, as an Art writer says, that 'the Venetians surpassed in colour because they worshipped God,' the French exhibit little sign of faith by this test. Eastern scenes are very popular, involving plenty of rich colouring and affording scope for dramatic effect. Thus we have 'Zara waiting for Muça' by the well in the cool courtyard; and, farther on, more daughters of Mahomet revelling in Eastern luxury; a carpeted terrace overlooking moonlit scenery, Chinese lanterns, laughing eyes, wicked looks, and stern and scowling despots. One large picture represents a disconsolate Peri at the gate of Eden; a fair and comely maiden standing with her hands crossed upon her breast, a rich Cashmere shawl encircling her waist, and a jewelled bracelet her arm; the conventional type of fair womanhood, but neither sorrowful, disconsolate, nor ethereal. The bracelet is wonderfully painted, the shawl looks as if it might be lifted off, and the 'door of Paradise' is a careful tracing of a Moresque doorway from the Alcazar at Seville.

At the well-appointed theatre there is a Parisian company performing in the lightest of comedies, but so easily and so well, that (when the curtain draws up, and two young people are discovered in confidential conversation) the three or four occupants of the stalls feel as if they were intruding on some private interview, and are half inclined to withdraw.

But we have perhaps detained the reader long enough at Toulouse, for we have failed to find (excepting in sculpture at the Musée) many great works either in art, architecture, science, or commerce; we depend upon its '*assocations monumentales*' for any abiding interest, and note in passing, that generally, both in the Pyrenees and in Spain, those objects which leave the most lasting impression on the mind are the relics of a former age and an alien nation—in the Pyrenees, those of the Romans, and in Spain, of the Moors.

Toulouse is in the centre of a district so rich in architectural remains, and in towns of historic interest, that the traveller may well hesitate as to the direction he should take when turning his steps homeward; to the antiquary, to the archæologist, and to the artist, we should not hesitate to say, visit Carcassone, Narbonne, and Nismes, three cities which are perfect museums in themselves.

The ancient towers of Carcassone will perhaps commend themselves more to the artist, and the museum at Narbonne to the antiquary; but no traveller can visit Nismes without feeling amply repaid. The mere mention of its chief attractions will be enough—the beautiful Corinthian 'Maison Carrée,' still in such delicate preservation, that it looks as if it ought to be covered with a house of glass; the ancient Amphitheatre (where bullfights are occasionally held and where in 1866 they killed a matador); and, eleven miles from the town, that noble monument of the Romans, the 'Pont du Gard,' that spans the valley with its three tiers of arches—an aqueduct 180 feet high and nearly 900 feet long.

There is another route from Toulouse to Paris in a northerly direction, by Aurillac and Clermont, to Vichy, which possesses the attraction of beautiful scenery, combined with the pleasure of getting somewhat off the beaten track, and which would enable us to see another French watering-place.

But we will now retrace our steps a little, taking the train to Tarbes and thence by diligence to Pau, passing

TARBES.

in the latter part of the journey through a district of undulating hills, tinted with pale yellow gorse, covered with heath and ferns in all stages of colour, and dotted with flocks of sheep; passing villages and *villageois*, dirty and poor-looking, the women roughly clothed, ragged, and unkempt; up hills so steep that oxen have to be yoked to the diligence to draw it; afterwards along dreary and monotonous roads with their two lines of poplar trees that give no shade, so flat and straight that they vanish over the horses' heads into the shape of a needle-point at the horizon of the plain—and so once more to the town of Pau.

Thence by railway, through Orthez again, to Bayonne, by the banks of the broad river Adour, losing altogether, in our rapid flight, the view of the old city and its fortifications that used to be obtained from the road when, descending the hill at the last few miles, we caught occasional glimpses of the sea and the distant mountains reaching far into Spain. Fortunate were we, then, if we were in time to see the sun set, before rumbling through the busy old town of Bayonne, 'une ville gaie, originale et demi-espagnole,' with its gables, fortifications, —and streets narrow

BAYONNE.

enough to remind one of Lawrence Sterne's wish that they might be a trifle wider, if only to be able to say on which side we are walking,—and so on to Biarritz, to take a last glimpse of the world of fashion disporting itself by the sea.

## CHAPTER XII.

### *BIARRITZ—ST. JEAN DE LUZ.*

THERE is a great stir and bustle in the town of Bayonne, for everybody is bent upon leaving it; the railway station is crowded, and every carriage and vehicle worthy of the name has its occupant. There are omnibuses and diligences loading in front of the Hotel, and in every part of the town we find the same movement seaward. There is a grand fête at Biarritz, and in spite of late storms and the still threatening aspect of the sky, every road that leads in the direction of the sea is thronged with a line of vehicles, and with the Basque peasantry on foot.

Biarritz, always gay and lively, and crowded with visitors in the season, is especially so to-day, when it is no easy matter to get accommodation; the hotels and lodging-houses near the sea are all occupied, and many travellers have to return at night to sleep at Bayonne. The distance from Bayonne to Biarritz is about five miles by the road, which many prefer to the railway, the greater part of the way being along a straight flat road lined with trees. A few minutes before we reach Biarritz, we pass on our right hand the private chapel of the late Empress, and the gates leading to the Villa Eugénie. The Villa itself we can see through the shrubbery, a plain substantial building close to the shore, but bare and bleak-looking, exposed on every side to the wind, although the shrubs and trees that were planted round it have grown up during the last two or three years, and give it more shelter on the land side than would

VILLA EUGENIE

appear from the illustration. It is the least picturesque and the bleakest spot in Biarritz, and almost the only one whence no good view of the Spanish mountains (just indicated in the sketch at the head of this chapter) can be obtained. These mountains are in fact part of the chain of the Pyrenees, extending westward.

The town of Biarritz consists of a number of irregularly-built white houses, several large hotels, and a casino. The chief streets are full of shops with Paris wares, fantastic bathing dresses, and Spanish wools. The promenades and walks by the sea and on the rocks literally swarm with people; amongst whom the fine tall figures and handsome faces of the Basque peasantry are conspicuous.

We who have seen so much gaiety of costume in the Pyrenees, will not be so much struck with the brilliant assemblage of visitors of all nations who crowd annually here, and amongst whom the late Empress of the French used to walk about in the afternoon almost unattended;

but we shall admire the beauty of the coast-line, the bold headlands and rocks where the sea has undermined it in places, leaving caverns and natural bridges in the cliff when the tide is out.

From the rocks and promontories we obtain beautiful views of the mountains stretching far away into Spain and losing themselves in the sea; and when the tide rises on stormy days, we get an idea of the danger of this iron-bound coast, and understand why there is little shipping in sight, and no harbour worthy of the name. There are curious nooks and crannies in the rocks, where the French have 'utilised' the caverns worn by the sea, and built cafés and a 'Parc aux huitres,' the oysters being brought here by railway from the north of France! They have also built a handsome Casino on the shore— a long white building of four stories facing the sea, where in the evenings and in wet weather visitors assemble. In this building there were the usual suite of rooms for reading, 'conversation,' billiard-playing, &c., and the 'Salon,' where they dance or listen to the band; but the real business of the place was conducted in a little room upstairs, the 'Salon de Jeu.' There was a business-like air about this quiet corner of the Casino which indicated very plainly that the interest in écarté was absorbing enough, and that, in spite of laws to the contrary, France manages to enjoy the pleasures of 'le jeu' undisturbed. We could comprehend better after paying a visit to the 'corner,' why the 'Salon de Société' was so dull, and why the reading-room (well supplied with newspapers) was generally empty.

There were balls and concerts nearly every evening for the select and wealthy part of the community; and a travelling circus and other amusements for the crowds that lingered about Biarritz until late into the night.

The Port Vieux is the principal bathing-place—a deep bay, with smooth sloping sands and high rocks on either side, which serve as a protection from the force of the waves, and keep the water tolerably smooth for swimmers. There is an 'Établissement,' a handsome wooden erection forming three sides of a square, fitted up for bathers, with galleries and seats for spectators, and a café and a band attached. These sands are the great rendezvous for visitors at Biarritz, and the great sight of the town at the hours of bathing; and at high water there are many favourable positions on the rocks above for watching the evolutions of the bathers, without joining the throng of people on the sands.

The French system of bathing 'en famille' is well known, and it differs little here from what we may see at Trouville or Étretat, only that the 'costumes de bain' are more varied, and the toilettes of the Spanish and French spectators are, if possible, more gay.

Let us join the crowd seated working and chatting on the beach, and note one or two characteristic figures. A tall object soon emerges from one of the doors of the 'Établissement' and walks slowly down, and as he passes we recognise a grave and somewhat portly gentleman, who sat near us at the table d'hôte at the 'Grand Hôtel;' but he is transformed into an acrobat, and his dignity has forsaken him. He resembles so exactly one of our street mountebanks, that we should not be surprised to see him spread a carpet on the sands and stand on his head. He stays for some time to chat with his family, who accompany him to the beach to see him make his first plunge, and who will afterwards join him in the water. Presently he wades into the sea, and clambering on to a rock, shrieks out something which we cannot catch the sense of, but which suffices to draw general attention to his movements, and, springing into the air, turns a somersault deftly, and 'flops' into the water like a great round ball. The children shriek with delight, and run off to the chalets to put on bathing-dresses. They soon return, the miniatures of their parent, and, having gourds fixed to their shoulders, they are put into the sea, and left to float about by themselves. The bay is soon filled with moving objects, of all shapes and sizes—dark shiny creatures crawling up the rocks, and others darting about in every direction—and resembles nothing so much as a gigantic aquarium.

But the gaiety of the party on the sands where the band is playing, and every chair is occupied to witness a singular *Bal de mer*, is the most attractive part of the show. Here is a group of four gentlemen who have just come down, surrounded by ladies, laughing, shouting, and talking at the top of their voices. Their costume has evidently been studied for effect, and it is but fair to say that they succeed in creating a sensation. One of the four especially, clad in a suit of green, resembled that quaint grasshopper-like figure that appeared some years ago at the *Théâtre du Châtelet* at Paris—Comète, the Bohemian dancer; like Comète, his legs were delightful, and the air with which he paced the sands before making the first plunge, would have been invaluable on the stage. The others were nearly as eccentric in appearance; and altogether, we can think of no human creatures with which to compare them (especially when all four join hands and rush into the water pell-mell), than a brilliant company of pantomimists.

We have scarcely noticed the ladies, who—having had a pail of fresh water poured over their heads as they stand on the beach in the most scanty description of 'bloomer' costume—are being towed or carried out to sea by their husbands or bathing-attendants; nor have we said anything of the number or skill of the swimmers. We will now go to the 'Côte des Fous,' where the bathers are more numerous, less select, not quite so particular about their costume, and a little more robust in their frolics.

In this more exposed part of the bay of Biarritz, the

Atlantic waves come in with a long unbroken sweep, and with a strength and weight which we can understand, by the distant booming sound against the rocks that guard the Port Vieux. It is no easy task for even a good swimmer to hold his own against the long sweep of one of these waves, which steals treacherously in, with scarcely a ripple on its surface until within a few feet of the shore, when it curls over in a mass of foam that makes it difficult to rise to, dragging the swimmer down as if in the clutches of the devil-fish in Victor Hugo's 'Toilers of the Sea.'[1]

But let us look at the company. There are at least a hundred bathers of both sexes in dark 'costumes de bain,' some creeping down the sands, five or six perhaps hand-in-hand, some racing, some turning somersaults; a grand levée of heads in the water, fifty or more romping together in one large circle; others dripping and shivering on the shore, a number of attendants to dip the timid or the weak, and a crowd of spectators on the sands. We have no fear of Mrs. Grundy's disapproval when we say that we joined the throng on the beach, for in truth the costumes of the bathers were often more 'comme il faut' than those on the shore, but we were curious to discover why so large a crowd had collected at this spot. We were not kept long in suspense; it was to see 'a wave come in.'

The storms of the previous days had greatly subsided; the sea was now comparatively smooth, and the sky clear overhead, but there remained a ground-swell, the like of which we had never witnessed before. Not very far out to sea we could distinguish, what first appeared to be a dark shadow on the water extending for some

---

[1] Many a stout swimmer has been carried under water by the treacherous strength of the under-current, or backwater, at Biarritz.

distance, which as it came nearer was evidently a long stretching wave coming ashore. We who are on the beach hear it striking the rocks and masonry of the breakwater, and can tell by the sudden rising of the water in that direction, that it must have filled the little bay at the Port Vieux, and put to flight all the fashionable coterie on the chairs in the Cave of Canute; it had done

this, and perhaps more—it may have fatally injured a few morning toilettes, but here the consequences are more ludicrous if less disastrous.

There are about fifty people now in the water, sixty or seventy feet from us, some swimming, some dipping, some being dipped, the majority standing up to their shoulders in the sea, when the wave comes down upon them. The bathing-men call out as usual for all to jump, or rise to it, but this time it is too high for them, and altogether too powerful and sudden. It breaks just over their heads with a fall of water of several feet, like innumerable cascades; engulfs the struggling, helpless mass of human beings in its foam, takes them up in its arms, and with a long sweep, or slide we should call it, runs them up the beach, and leaves them struggling in a confused heap upon the shore far away from the sea, breathless and bewildered, but more frightened than hurt. The spectators rush to the rescue, and crowd round the heap to pick out their friends, forming a picture on the sands that we will not attempt to describe; we can only compare it to a common event on the sea-shore, when a fisherman empties his nets, and the people collect round him to divide the spoil. The simile may be uncomplimentary but it is not far-fetched, for in such straits, and in such costumes, there is little difference between human creatures and little fishes.

There were several stormy days at Biarritz, succeeded at last by one of those delightful balmy days peculiar to the South of France, when the 'light wind plays upon the land and upon the sea,' when all nature is in harmony, and everything living seems to rejoice. On such a day we charter a little basket-carriage, to take our last drive, to visit the neighbouring smuggling village of St. Jean de Luz. We keep near the sea nearly all the way, obtaining fresh views of the Spanish coast, and of the rocks which guard the shore: enjoying the soft air which breathes across the bay, where—

> 'Tides of grass break into foam of flowers,
> And the wind's feet shine along the sea.'

We find this little town, that has been making desperate attempts during the last few years to vie with Biarritz, now almost deserted, hotels closing, the casino on its last legs, the fishermen returning to their occupations, and mending their sails on the sea-shore. We

' Sweet day, so calm, so cool, so bright,
　The bridal of the earth and sky,
The dews shall weep thy fall to-night—
　For thou must die ! '

account for the flitting of the gay population, partly from the recent bad weather, and partly from the statement in a Biarritz newspaper, that 'Tous les baigneurs qui reviennent de Saint-Jean de Luz déclarent que ce pays n'offre aucune distraction ; de tous côtés l'on fait des plaintes contre le Casino, la musique est mauvaise et le service très mal fait.'[1]

The attractions of St. Jean de Luz, fortunately for us, are natural, and do not depend upon the Casino or 'la

musique,' and we can well spend the remainder of the day upon the sea-shore. The storms that break upon this exposed coast with such fearful violence that more than a hundred houses have been undermined or destroyed, is succeeded by a calm that nothing can exceed in beauty as evening approaches. The sea of sapphire and beryl that has been lying smooth and still for the

---

[1] As a matter of fact this paragraph is a little unfair ; St. Jean de Luz has much to recommend it, the good inns and bathing establishments being altogether quieter and more reasonable than Biarritz. August 1880.

last two hours under a cloudless sky, changes to a darker tone; scarce a ripple comes into the bay, or a breath of wind over the wide waters; only one little fishing-boat, with her graceful drooping sail (casting a faint shadow as she crosses the sun), drops into the silvery bay—silvery now from the moon's rays cast upon the shore.

At Biarritz and St. Jean de Luz we take leave of our friends, some returning to England, some going to Mentone, and some to Spain. The conversation, at Biarritz, had often turned upon the practicability of making an expedition into the interior of a country, of which attractive glimpses had been obtained from the 'Ports' of the Pyrenees. The majority of travellers content themselves with a visit to St. Sebastian, which cannot be said to give much insight into the character of the country or people, and has extorted from many a solemn vow never to go a step farther into Spain.

There is a halo of mystery and romance still clinging to the peninsula, that many would not care to dispel; but for those who are anxious to see the land of Don Quixote, and to become acquainted with the people, there is nothing that need deter them. Notwithstanding the never-to-be-forgotten testimony of Miss Eyre, it is quite possible for ladies to travel on the high roads unattended.

We have lately met two English ladies who made the tour of the north of Spain without escort, and without experiencing any of those annoyances or mishaps of which the public has heard so much. For the benefit of future travellers, it is worth while to state what they did. Entering Spain by Irun and St. Sebastian, they went to Burgos by railway and thence to Madrid. They visited the Escorial and Toledo, Saragossa and

Barcelona, and returned to the Pyrenees by Perpignan and Toulouse. Travelling always in the compartment reserved for *Señoras* on railways, keeping rigidly to the high roads, and stopping only at large towns, they found it for the most part 'plain-sailing,' and thoroughly enjoyed the journey. Without knowing anything of the Spanish language, they did what any two ladies might do again, with perfect propriety and safety—accomplish, unattended, one of the most interesting tours in Europe. They said it was 'very expensive,' but that they did not seem to mind. Their great secret was, that they were well provided for the journey both positively and negatively; they travelled with plenty of money, without prejudice, and without a dog.

A few words in conclusion. If it be thought that, in the preceding pages, we have not given sufficient illustrations of costume, or said enough about the people, the answer is, that in a journey of this kind we come very little into contact with the peasantry. Nothing is more curious, when looking back upon scenes visited over and over again, than to find how very slight an impression the inhabitants and their doings have made upon the mind, and considering the extent of country visited, how few inhabitants were seen. It is not because the bent of M. Doré's genius has led him to endow the rocks and trees with an almost human interest, that we have in sympathy thought more of these, but because, after spending months in the mountains, of the residents we have very little to record.

Of the animals in the Pyrenees there is also little to be said. Wolves are rarely met with, poison having been made use of to exterminate them. There are a few bears to be found in winter; in summer we see only the dancing specimen sketched on p. 110. The izard (*Antelope rupicapra*) may often be found on the higher mountains; they are shot and brought down to the hotels to serve as a delicacy at table. Foxes are often seen scampering on ahead of the traveller as he climbs the rocks. Eagles (the finest of which is the *Gypaetus barbatus*) and vultures, are only seen at great heights, near the snow-line. Buzzards (*la Buse*) make their appearance in parties and settle on the trees near the plains; they are of remarkable size. There are a few pheasants, some trout in the lakes, and red-legged partridges in the Landes. The ermine has been taken in the snow at Luchon close to the village in the winter; specimens may be seen in M. Lézat's stuffed collection at Luchon. The most beautiful domestic animal is the Pyrenean dog, he is generally large, with long white or cream-coloured hair, and eyes and ears like a mastiff; a magnificent creature, whom, as some one says, 'it is an honour to know.' There is a fine specimen at the Hôtel du Parc at Cauterets.

In landscape-painting, where figures have to be introduced, the artist will find (as in the Val d'Ossau) nothing more suitable or characteristic than the field women in their white capulets, tending the fawn-coloured cattle; and at a distance it matters little that their picturesqueness is the result of tatters rather than of taste. A step higher in the social scale, and nearly everything like distinctive costume has vanished in the Pyrenees, and our interest in it at the same ratio. But if the natives will doff their pretty head-dresses, and take to Lyons bonnets and Manchester cottons, the visitors, as we have often explained, help to make up for the deficiency by the fancifulness of their attire; and of all modern head-dresses, none are more effective or becoming than the bright woollen head-dress that only a

Bigorre peasant woman knows how to make, and only a Frenchwoman knows how to wear.

We have alluded already to the comparatively small number of English people who travel in the Pyrenees; but as we have perhaps more American than English readers, we may ask the question, 'How it comes to pass' that, when the American people think it worth while to pay a visit to Europe, almost exclusively to see Paris, Switzerland and Italy, so few should think it worth while to come to the Pyrenees? The feast is provided— where are the guests? These mountains form one of the loveliest gardens in Europe and a perfect place for a summer holiday—' la beauté ici est sereine et le plaisir est pur.'

# POSTSCRIPT.

### SPRING IN THE PYRENEES, AMONGST THE FLOWERS.

FROM a visitor at Argelès, we gather some notes of flowers; notes made in the freshness of spring-time, before the heat and clatter of the season have begun. They will be interesting to botanical readers, and to many who have only seen the Pyrenees in the autumn.

ARGELÈS.—In May and June we found the valley of Argelès a paradise of flowers; the meadows were nearly all flowers, they were lying thickly also under the poplars, and the low stone walls full of ferns. The meadows were yellow with rattle, mixed with every shade of purple orchis, from pure white, through mauve, to deepest purple. In shady corners *Geranium phæum* grew large and velvety, of a rich red brown. Blue geraniums and columbines filled the fields, showing more brilliantly on these grassy slopes than in our home gardens. Beside the streams we found *Thalictrum aquilegifolium*, the flowers of which have a soft but faded appearance; *Thalictrum minus* also. On the walls and rocks were hepaticas, white and blue, and a variety of sedums decorating the stones with their blossoms and leaves of coral and greyish green; the monastery of Pocy La Hun is bright with them in June.

On the hill-sides opposite Argelès were beds of *Primula farinosa*, delicate pink and lilac, set in moss; also *Gentiana acaulis* and *verna*. Above was the snow, and where it had melted in patches we found the beautiful little *Ranunculus pyrenæus*, common in the higher Alps, and from the hills above Argelès came our first bouquet of the alpine rose.

In the woods we found Star of Bethlehem, but as a rule there are not many flowers in these woods; the chestnut woods are carpeted with the finest turf, soft and dry; green alleys, delightful to wander in, on a hot morning.

CAUTERETS.—The rocks in this gorge are covered in early summer with bushes of white heath, and in the ledges are purple *pinguicula;* the natives call them violets. The purple and white *Erinus* grows nearly everywhere on these rocks, and, on the bridges which span the streams, hangs the *Linaria alpina*. In these gorges we find the well-known *Raimondia pyrenaica*, growing in tufts on the higher ledges of the rocks (a purple flower with golden centre, named after Raimond the botanist, the wonder of the traveller to Gavarnie), which guides gather for travellers. Here also is the grass of Parnassus and *Iberis*, or candy-tuft, a pincushion-like plant of *Saxifraga aretioides*, which bears heads of yellow flowers on red stems. Another little plant to notice here and at Bagnères de Bigorre is the *Fritillaria pyrenaica*.

GAVARNIE.—On the road to Gavarnie are fields full of daffodils. Passing through the wonderful 'Chaos,' we saw no plants excepting a few small ferns; but the basin of the Cirque is a perfect garden. All the flowers of Argelès, and more, are here; the *Soldanella*, a delicate little plant, described by Ruskin ('Modern Painters,' vol. ii. p. 84), and *Dryas octopetala* in blossom. Here we dug up some iris bulbs, a blue kind which does well in England; also the scaly bulb of the large squill, a handsome example of which was found at the foot of the Cirque precipices, almost touching the snow. There was also plenty of the *Saxifraga longifolia* growing in crevices of the high rocks.

BAGNÈRES DE BIGORRE.—This town is very pleasant in spring; the hills around are easily accessible, lacets being cut in the steep slopes. The mountain-tops are limestone, but the higher and barer the rocks, the more thickly do brightly coloured flowers grow out of all the holes and crevices. On Mont Né were the finest beds of *Gentiana acaulis* we had yet seen, set in moss between large stones.

LUCHON.—Here we found fresh varieties of flowers. By the roadsides was the small red *Saponaria*, and in the first grass-fields we passed was the silvery *Astrantia major*, growing luxuriantly in branched specimens more than two feet high. There are fine plants of this on the river Pique. Near Luchon we found the two blue *Phyteumas* (*spicatum* and *orbiculare*), and the smaller butterfly orchis on the slopes below the Tour de Castel Vieil; a little further up the road towards the Vallée du Lys the meadows were full of *Narcissus poeticus*, growing as thickly as our English daffodils. The VALLÉE DU LYS ends in a sort of 'cirque' or amphitheatre of rocks, approached by a steep winding path (*see Illustration, p.* 191). The rocks and precipices are clothed with beeches and firs, underneath which are natural rockeries, well stocked with ferns, saxifrages and sedums. The oak and beech ferns are wonderfully green, living in the spray of the torrents. Here we find the lily (*Anthericum liliastrum*) from which the valley takes its name, called in England St. Bruno's lily. Those who have seen it only in the herbaceous border, cannot realise its beauty in groups in the long grass. The buds are tinged with pale green, and the open flowers are almost transparent, white with yellow stamens. The lily family is well represented in the Pyrenees; near the Pont du Roi, in a pass leading into Spain, we saw high above our heads plants of the orange pompone lily in blossom. The fields near Luchon are full of a gay little single pink; another flower which looks well in the meadows is the pink *Anthyllis*. Hereabout we found *Arnica*, quantities of which are offered for sale in the avenue at Luchon, also a crimson-clustered pink, like a wild sweet-william.

On the ENTÉCADE leading into Spain (*see Map*) we found daffodils again (although we were now well into July), quantities of dog's-tooth violets, and beds of *Sempervivum*; but the prettiest thing was *Androsace carnea*, with its moss-like leaves and charming pink blossoms. Coming down we found plenty of *Ranunculus amplexicaulis*, pale pink with large bluish leaves, also a brilliant forget-me-not, which only grows on high ground, and *Daphne cneorum*. The soldanella was here, also the *Viola cornuta*; sometimes a grass-field will be quite coloured with the beautiful pale purple flowers of the latter.

One of the most desolate spots near Luchon is the LAC D'OO, but the steep and stony path leading up to it is enlivened by bushes of *Rhododendron ferrugineum*, or *rose des Alpes*, in full blossom between the grey rocks. Here we made a bouquet of *white* flowers picked near Super-Bagnères—lilies of the valley, the cream-coloured *Anemone narcissiflora*, *Anemone pulsatilla*, silky and grey outside; a large white anemone with pale blue outside; *Ranunculus amplexicaulis*, *aconitifolium*, and *pyrenæus*; with the *Anthericum* peculiar to the Vallée du Lys; all set in the great leaves of the lily of the valley.

BIARRITZ.—The flat country round would be uninteresting but for the abundant and brightly-coloured flowers; the brightest of all is a local plant, the *fleur des frontières* (or *grémil couché*), a lapis-lazuli blue, just tinged with red, sometimes spoken of by travellers erroneously as a gentian. It grows here on barren wastes and near roadside hedges, but we never met with it elsewhere in the Pyrenees. Another roadside flower is a large white cistus with a yellow centre, looking at a distance like a wild white rose. On the rocks washed by the waves are the cistus, the pale pink thrift, and the yellow everlasting. On the sands are fringed pinks and *Convolvulus soldanella*, growing beside a land stream, between the stones. Other flowers, such as the horned poppy, grow on this windy shore just out of reach of the waves.

At Biarritz, one of the prettiest sights was a profusion of pink and deep red *Cephalanthera* growing in the long grass near the neglected grounds of the Villa Eugénie. One plant peculiar to this district is a star-like white flower, purple outside, with lily-like stem, *Simethis bicolor*. It is found in the woods near Biarritz; fresh stars shine from it every day. Here also is the king-spear (*Asphodel ramosum*), which grows throughout the Pyrenees.

The above will serve as an indication to those who care for flowers, of what may be found in the most accessible parts of the Pyrenees. Fern collectors and botanists will do well to take Mr. Packe's 'Guide to the Pyrenees' (Longmans, 1867). There is general information in it not to be found elsewhere, including a description of forty-two species of ferns.

The variety and beauty of the flowers, and the luxuriant ferns, give a special character to these valleys, which we commend to the attention of artists. The vineyards are very unlike those in the plains of France; here cherries and maples are planted for the support of the vines, the twisted stems of which cling round the cherry trees, and half conceal them with their foliage, stretching out graceful arms from tree to tree. The thick beech woods are most beautiful in June, the oaks are then just coming out into red leaf; above are the fir forests, composed principally of silver fir and spruce, and last of all, rocky peaks covered with snow.

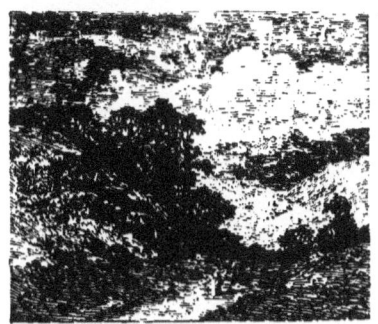

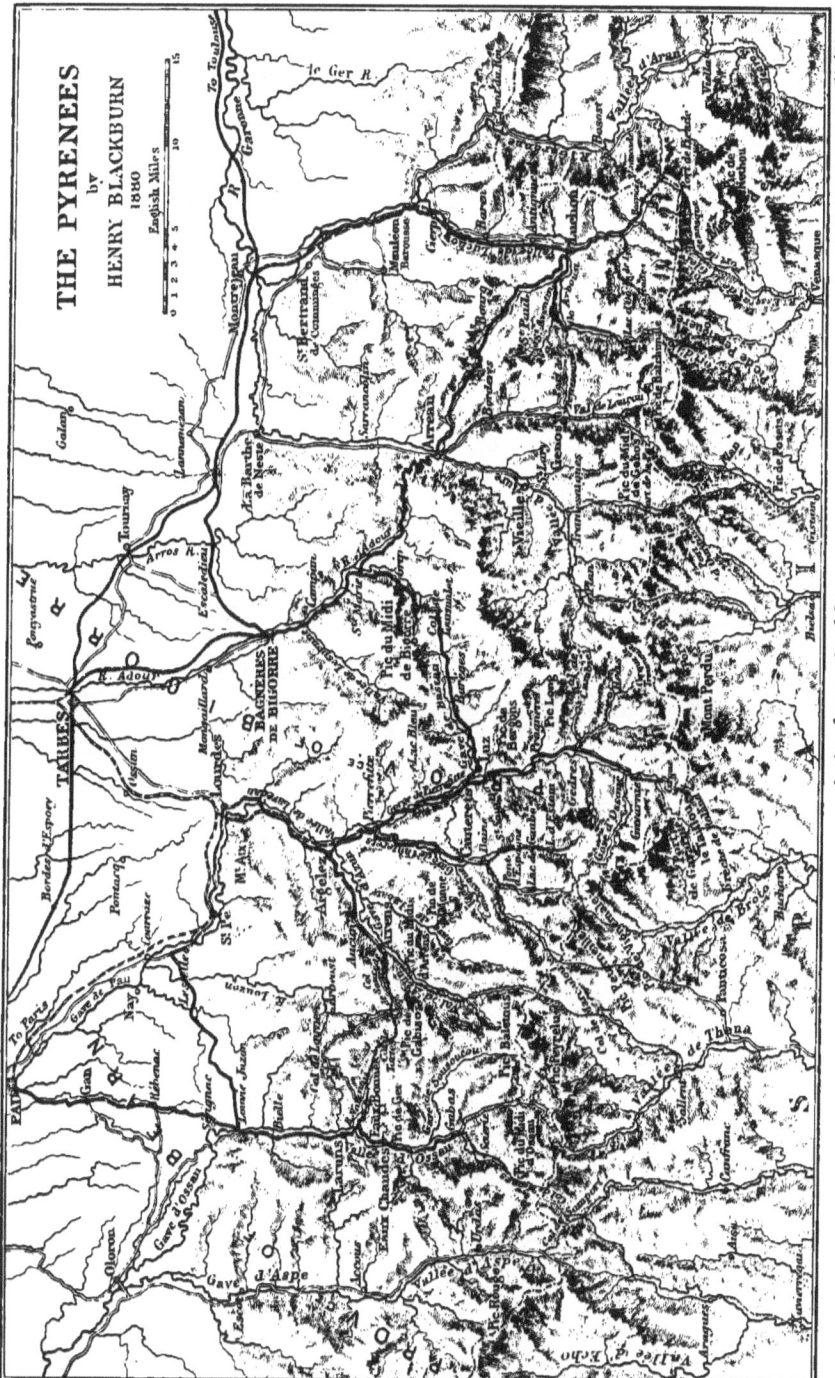

# APPENDIX

OF

# INFORMATION FOR TRAVELLERS.

**Pau** (Pop. 30,000). Season, autumn, winter and spring; a fine protected situation with mild climate; hot in July and August, when tourists visit the city. Good houses and apartments to be let, and good hotels; but Pau is not a cheap place of residence in winter. There is good society, English, French and Spanish; hunting, shooting, fishing, steeple-chasing, polo, &c. English churches and club. Soft still air; few mosquitoes. Ry. to Paris, Bayonne, &c.

(HOTELS.) Grand, Beau Séjour (fine situation), France, Paix, Angleterre, &c. Good pension, 8 to 10 francs, generally excellent.

    [**Pau to Eaux-Chaudes.** Dil. 27 miles. (Railway making, 1880); passing **Laruns**. Hotels: Touristes, Voyageurs, &c.]

**Eaux-Chaudes** (Height 2215 ft.). A small village built on a stream in a gorge, with Thermal Establishment, and limited accommodation for patients. Six sulphureous springs, 95° Fahr. Swimming and other baths. Romantic, gloomy situation, the sun disappearing at 3.30 p.m. in summer. Living is cheaper here than at Eaux-Bonnes. The waters recommended for consumptive patients. A good situation from which to make excursions on the mountains.

(HOTELS.) Baudot, France, Angleterre, &c. Pension, 7 and 8 fr.; fairly good; short summer season.

    [**Eaux-Chaudes to Eaux-Bonnes.** 4 miles, omnibus daily.]

**Eaux-Bonnes** (Height 2454 ft.). A street of large, well-built modern hotels and lodging-houses, crowded on a ledge cut in the rock, shaded by trees. Season, June to October. Good Établissement; seven warm sulphureous springs, the hottest 91° Fahr.; stronger than at Eaux-Chaudes. Many fashionable and consumptive patients. Lodgings dear in July and August. Meals supplied from restaurants, 5 to 8 fr. a day; a more civilised residence than Eaux-Chaudes.

(HOTELS.) France, Prince's, Richelieu, &c. Pension, 8 to 12 fr.

    [**Eaux-Bonnes to Argelès**, fine mountain road, 27 miles. Dil. daily in summer; or return to Pau, and by Ry. viâ **Lourdes**. Hotels: Pyrenees France, &c.]

**Argelès** (Pop. 1800. Height 1790 ft.). A pleasant village in fine scenery, 9 miles from Lourdes; central for excursions, but rather hot in summer, owing to protected situation. Good head-quarters for an artist, or a botanist; some shooting and fishing. No invalids at Argelès. English chaplain in summer.

(HOTELS.) France (very comfortable), Angleterre, &c., open all the year. Good pension, 3 meals with wine and service, 8 fr.

> [**Argelès to Cauterets,** 11 miles. Ry. as far as **Pierrefitte,** 4 miles. (Hotels: Poste, Pyrenees, &c.) Here the Ry. ends, and travellers are beset by beggars and touters for carriages, &c. It is better to take carriage at Argelès.]

**Cauterets** (Pop. in summer, 4000 to 5000; Height 3254 ft.). An important Pyrenean spa on the mountains, with upwards of 250 houses; paved streets, a market and octroi, good hotels and lodgings. Season, June to September; climate bracing owing to height, but *rainy*. Numerous hot sulphureous springs, 102° to 140° Fahr., much resorted to for rheumatism, also for throat affections. Large Établissement and casino. Every convenience for invalids, including sedan chairs. Cauterets is hot, fashionable and amusing in July and August; a favourite resort of French and Spaniards. Fine excursions.

(HOTELS.) France and Angleterre (excellent), Ambassadeurs, &c. Good pension, 10 fr.; accommodation to suit all purses.

> [**Cauterets to St. Sauveur (and Luz,** Hotel: Pyrenees, good and reasonable, Univers, &c.), viâ Pierrefitte, 15 miles; or over the mountains 4 to 5 hours, guide not necessary.]

**St. Sauveur** (Height 2310 ft.). A street of about fifty white houses built on the ledge of a mountain near the Gave, one mile from Luz; closed in late autumn on account of snow. Good Établissement with sulphureous springs, weaker than at Cauterets. It is called the "Ladies' Watering-place;" formerly much frequented by the late Empress of the French. Pleasant walks in the neighbourhood of St. Sauveur and Luz. Apartments to be had at both places, and guides for the mountains.

(HOTELS.) France, Prince's, &c. Accommodation limited.

> [**St. Sauveur to Gavarnie,** 12 miles, carriage-road (viâ Gèdres, 7 miles; small inn). Gavarnie (4380 ft.). Here is a tolerable mountain inn; one night at least should be spent at Gavarnie in summer.]
>
> [**Luz to Barèges,** 4¼ miles, good carriage-road.]

**Barèges** (Height 4084 ft.). About eighty houses built up on the steep banks of the Gave, shut in by mountains; a bleak and misty place, crowded in summer and in winter deserted; not attractive to visitors, but celebrated for its curative waters. Établissement with resident

# APPENDIX.

physician; strong sulphureous springs. Here is a Hospital with several hundred invalids, wounded soldiers and Government employés. (HOTELS.) Europe, France, &c. Good accommodation dear at Barèges.

[**Barèges to Bagnères de Bigorre,** by the Tourmalet, 25 miles; steep carriage-road, available only in summer. 15 miles on the way is Gripp (Hotel, Voyageurs), thence by a good road to Bagnères.]

**Bagnères de Bigorre** (Pop. 10,000; Height 1814 ft.). An ancient town, much visited in the summer for the bathing, and drinking the waters. Bagnères is a pleasant sheltered place in winter, with a temperature less variable than most of the watering-places. Reasonable apartments; a good market and cheap provisions. Établissement and Pump-room; iron and saline springs, 87° to 123° Fahr., recommended for their tonic qualities and in nervous affections; but not for serious complaints. English church, club and casino; fishing and shooting. English and French society. Good head-quarters; horses and guides for excursions. See relief map of mountains by M. Frossard.

(HOTELS.) Paris (good and clean in 1880), Londres, Beau Séjour, &c., all reasonable. Pension, 7 and 8 fr. most of the year.

[**Bigorre to Luchon,** by Ry. viâ **Tarbes** Jn. (Hotel, Ambassadeurs); or over the Col d'Aspin by **Arreau** (Hotel, d'Angleterre, comfortable), 8 to 10 hours.]

**Luchon** (Pop. in summer, 5000 to 6000; Height 2064 ft.). The most frequented of the Pyrenean watering-places; old and new town, well situated in a broad valley, surrounded by mountains. Excellent Établissement and casino, and fine hotels; very lively and crowded in the season, July and August. Warm sulphureous springs, 82° to 150° Fahr., celebrated for cures of rheumatic and cutaneous disorders. Here are the comforts of life as at Cauterets, and prices to correspond. It is a good place to visit in the height of summer for making excursions in the neighbourhood; many French and Spaniards come here who are not invalids. Season, 15th June to 15th October. Good libraries and shops. See the relief maps by M. Lézat in the Établissement.

(HOTELS.) Grand, Richelieu, Angleterre, des Bains, &c. Good pension, 8 to 10 fr.

[Ry. to **Toulouse** 87 miles, viâ **St. Bertrand de Comminges** (Hôtel de Comminges).]

**Toulouse** (Pop. 132,000), the ancient capital of Languedoc; a busy city situated in a plain on the Garonne, full of antiquarian interest; dull, provincial and cheap as a place of residence, rather hot in summer.

Environs not interesting ; good markets ; fiacres 90c. a course. Museum, library and club.

(HOTELS.) Tivollier, Souville, Europe, &c.

**Bayonne** (Pop. 28,000). A fortified town, on the high road and Ry. to Spain, commanding the western end of the Pyrenees. Bayonne is well situated on the Nive and the Adour; much commerce and shipping. Ry. and road to Biarritz, 5 miles.

(HOTELS.) Ambassadeurs, St. Étienne, Commerce, &c.

**Biarritz** (Pop. 6000 to 7000). A gay and fashionable watering-place, good sea bathing, mild climate, invigorating air; summer season May to October, crowded in July and August. A winter resort for English, who board comfortably at the hotels. English club, hunting and shooting. Ry. to St. Jean de Luz, 5 miles.

(HOTELS.) Grand, Angleterre, France, Paris, &c. Good pension in winter, 7 to 10 fr.

**St. Jean de Luz** (Pop. 4500). A good bathing-place frequented by Spaniards; environs more interesting than at Biarritz.

(HOTELS.) La Plage (new and good 1880), France, Poste, &c.

The Expenses of a 'tour in the Pyrenees' slightly exceed those of a similar journey to Switzerland, on account of the greater distance traversed, from England; the cost of living being about the same. Hotels and carriages are dear in July and August, and cheap in October; the latter being often the finest month in the year for the mountains. There are slow diligences on all the high roads, at the usual low fares. Carriages are expensive to hire for two people, but reasonable for a party of four or five. The tariff is 40 fr. a day with four horses, but an arrangement can be made at a lower rate for the whole tour of the Pyrenees.

A tour of one month costs each person from London, on the average, £50; and one of two months, £80. The journey may be accomplished for less, but will probably cost more in the height of the season.

In the map the reader will find the principal roads and mountain-paths accurately marked, but every pedestrian should provide himself with Packe's pocket 'Guide to the Pyrenees' (Longmans). Murray's Handbook for the South of France and the 'Guide Johanne' (Hachette) give full information for ordinary travellers.

*London, October,* 1880.

*Books by the same Author.*

'*ARTISTS AND ARABS.*'
'*TRAVELLING IN SPAIN.*'
'*NORMANDY PICTURESQUE.*'
'*THE HARZ MOUNTAINS.*'
'*BRETON FOLK.*'
'*THE STORY OF THE PASSION PLAY,*' *ETC.*

*Published by* SAMPSON LOW & *Co.*
Crown Buildings, Fleet Street, London.

*BY THE SAME AUTHOR.*

THIRD THOUSAND.

*Just published, imperial 8vo., cloth extra,* 21s.

# Breton Folk:

## An Artistic Tour in Brittany.

WITH ONE HUNDRED AND SEVENTY ILLUSTRATIONS
BY RANDOLPH CALDECOTT.

A NEW MAP OF ROUTES, AND INFORMATION FOR TRAVELLERS.

LONDON: SAMPSON LOW, MARSTON, SEARLE, & RIVINGTON.
1880.

[OVER.

## Opinions of the Press on 'Breton Folk.'

"This handsome volume is the result of a three years' tour in Brittany by Mr. Henry Blackburn, who was accompanied for two seasons by Mr. Randolph Caldecott. The tourist who intends to visit Brittany might do much worse than take this joint production of Messrs. Blackburn and Caldecott with him; not only will he find pleasure in its literary and artistic merits, but he will learn from its pages a quantity of general information about the country. He will learn about hotels and their charges, routes and conveyances, the rivers that may be fished in, and the country that may be shot over. Mr. Caldecott's sketches are characterised by discrimination, humour, and clever drawing; he has caught the principal characteristics of the Breton, man, woman, and child, with great felicity."—**Standard.**

"Messrs. Blackburn and Caldecott have been over the greater part of Brittany, and they have made the journey nearly always with freshness of interest, mind and eye. The excellence of the book is the result of this. Mr. Blackburn's information in 'Breton Folk' is not hackneyed, and Mr. Caldecott's illustrations give us a very true revelation of Breton character and of Breton scenery."—**Academy.**

"'Breton Folk' is the pleasant result of an artistic tour in Brittany * * * To say that the volume contains one hundred and seventy drawings by Mr. Caldecott is perhaps to say enough, for no contemporary artist combines so much truth with such unstrained and unaffected humour. Here, in short, is the whole life of the people displayed, ut in votiva tabella. Mr. Blackburn's part of the book is so good, and written in a style so pleasant and unforced, that the work is that very rare thing—a Christmas book which may be, and should be, read with serious attention."—**Saturday Review.**

"The 'Artistic Tour in Brittany' is a brilliant and sparkling work. The text has been written with good taste, and Mr. Caldecott has contributed a large number of spirited illustrations."—**Guardian.**

"Artist and author tracked the peasant in all parts of Brittany, exploring the out of the way nooks and corners unknown to tourists, and the harvest of their travels may be ranked as one of the brightest and most original volumes on Brittany."—**Graphic.**

"Mr. Caldecott's illustrations are natural and humorous, and Mr. Blackburn shows at every turn that he has caught, as few travellers could catch, the genius of the life of a people from whom the charm of primitiveness has not yet departed."—**World.**

"Written with a fresh and joyous touch, charmingly suggestive of a careless holiday, and illustrated with rare delicacy and humour, this choicely printed volume deserves a foremost place amongst the art-books of the season."—**Truth.**

"The text of 'Breton Folk' is as interesting as any novel."—**Scotsman.**

Etc. etc.

*BY THE SAME AUTHOR.*

*Just published, crown* 8vo., *cloth,* 10s. 6d.

# ART IN THE MOUNTAINS.

PHARISEE.

# The Story of the Passion Play.

*WITH NUMEROUS ILLUSTRATIONS,*

PROGRAMMES OF THE SCENES AND TABLEAUX, &c., &c.

LONDON: SAMPSON LOW, MARSTON, SEARLE, & RIVINGTON.
1880.

[OVER.

## Opinions of the Press on 'Art in the Mountains';
### THE STORY OF THE 'PASSION PLAY.'

" *Mr. Henry Blackburn gives us an account of the* ' *Passion Play*,' *that is acted once in every ten years at Oberammergau. He writes in excellent taste, and is interesting from the first page to the last; in fact, we must confess that, when once we had taken up his work, we did not lay it down until we had finished it. He has acquired the real art of brief writing, for he can say all that he himself wishes to say, and can leave unsaid all that the reader does not care to know.*"—Saturday Review.

" *In this volume we have an account of a tour of a comparatively unknown part of Germany, endued with all the local colour and picturesque description of which the author is a master, while the chronicle of the* '*Play*' *is a specimen of what may be called* '*theatrical criticism*,' *which might well be read by those who study ordinary stage performances.*"—Morning Post.

" *Mr. Henry Blackburn tells the story of the strange* '*Passion Play*' *at Oberammergau in his own pleasant way. The book is to be praised as a book of the best class and a valuable elucidation of an interesting topic.*"—Examiner.

" *Of the many previous accounts of the* '*Play*,' *none, we are disposed to think, recalls that edifying and impressive spectacle with the same clearness and vividness as Mr. Blackburn's volume;* \* \* \* *few writers, indeed, are so well capable of making text and illustrations work harmoniously together.*"—Guardian.

" *We especially wish to do justice to the literary merit of this work, because our opinion of the* '*Play*' *does not coincide with Mr. Blackburn's.*"—Record.

" *Mr. Blackburn's volume is the work of a true artist, devoted to his art and following it from pure love; he tells the story with remarkable grace, and throws a novel and thorough light upon the* '*Passion Play.*'"—Press.

" *Mr. Blackburn's charming volume tells the story of the* '*Play*' *so well, and his illustrations bring the actors so vividly before our eyes, that it cannot fail to please. The descriptions are remarkably graceful and artistic.*"—Observer.

" *This volume is as welcome as if the* '*Passionsspiel*' *were a new interest. The scenes are described with inimitable grace.*"—Lloyd's Newspaper.

" *Those who would like to possess a memorial of this strange* '*Play*' *cannot do better than make themselves possessors of this book.*"—Standard.

" *There is a tendre about this book like the delicacy of beautiful china, and a feeling of religion, without the slightest suspicion of obtrusion.*"—Publisher's Circular.

" *Mr. Blackburn regards the divine comedy as a poet and an artist, and aids his narrative with charming illustrations.*"—Globe.

*Etc. etc.*

www.ingramcontent.com/pod-product-compliance
Lightning Source LLC
Chambersburg PA
CBHW032002230426
43672CB00010B/2237